JEFFERSONIAN PRINCIPLES

EXTRACTS FROM THE
WRITINGS OF THOMAS JEFFERSON

Selected and Edited by

JAMES TRUSLOW ADAMS, LL.D., Litt.D.

BOSTON
LITTLE, BROWN, AND COMPANY
1928

Copyright, 1928,
BY JAMES TRUSLOW ADAMS

———

All rights reserved

Published March, 1928

INTRODUCTION

THE extracts gathered in this small volume are intended to illustrate the mind and not the life of Thomas Jefferson. They are not meant to be a footnote to history or to biography. The attempt has been made to select from Jefferson's writings those passages which give expression to his more general thoughts on politics, government, religion, education, and the art of living. Some of these expressions are found linked with great occasions, as in the Declaration of Independence or his First Inaugural as President, though such occasions did not always call forth such generalizations. At other times they occur in personal letters in connection with minor matters in Jefferson's own life or that of the nation. It will thus be found that a number of important events or decisions are not even mentioned here, such as Jefferson's Embargo policy. Had the intention been to explain his actions at important crises or to trace the intellectual background of his action through life, the choice would have had to be made on a wholly different system. It is hoped, however,

INTRODUCTION

that the selections may give the reader a clear notion of such fundamental ideas and principles as formed the foundation for all Jefferson's actions, so far as a statesman can guide himself in all details of practical life by the ideals of which he approves. Every public man in high office has been confronted from time to time by conditions which have necessitated compromise, not involving personal honor but involving what critics who have never themselves been placed in similar situations may consider as time-serving reversals of general principles to meet the exigencies of particular instances. As this volume is not biographical, it is no part of the editor's task to narrate or appraise the public services of Jefferson, but merely to elucidate, to some extent, his expressed philosophy and opinions.

In Jefferson's political thinking the fundamental postulate was his belief in the latent honesty and ability of the average man, of man as man, regardless of social position, education, wealth, or other opportunities. Take away this corner stone of his beliefs and all the rest of the structure falls to the ground. It must not be thought, however, in spite of the "glittering generalities" of the Declaration of Independence,

INTRODUCTION

that Jefferson thought that all men, under all conditions, exhibited these qualities sufficiently to make them capable of the self-governing system he conceived as the best for them when at their best themselves. He distinctly avowed the contrary in speaking of the peoples of certain other countries. He also prophesied that, should the open spaces of America be filled up and the people turn from agriculture to industrialism in crowded cities, they would then become corrupt as in other lands. Moreover, he admitted, by implication, that even in the agricultural United States of his day the people would not always be right. His theory of majority rule implied that there might be a very large minority of the people who might decide questions wrongly. Indeed, when speaking of the necessity of protecting the rights of the minority, he again implies that even the majority of the people might decide wrongly. He had spent years in France when the French Revolution was brewing. He had followed its subsequent course closely. He also knew the frontiersmen, slaves, and lower town-classes of his own country. He never enunciated the belief that under any and all circumstances *vox populi* must of necessity be *vox Dei*.

What he did claim, however, was that man inherently possesses the qualities which make him capable of self-government, that when he exhibits those qualities he should be allowed to govern himself, and that, in the America of his own day, the Americans of most classes did exhibit those qualities and were entitled to self-government. It was in these general and specific beliefs and his willingness to put them into practice that he differed from most of the statesmen of his time.

It was the belief in the inherent capacity of man as man to be, under the right conditions, a rational and right-willing creature, which led him to certain other beliefs. The first of these was that, as far as possible and as rapidly as possible, the right conditions should be brought about and the capacities of all men developed. Clearly servitude should be done away with, and Jefferson was a lifelong opponent of African slavery. He realized that for the good of both races emancipation must be gradual and he did his best to bring it about. In this he failed, almost by accident, and in the absence of any general change in condition he well understood that for the most part individual slaves freed in the South would not be better but worse off and that to sell his own to another man would merely deprive them of a good master for an uncertain fate. The fact that, under the conditions, he continued to own slaves himself does not invalidate the sincerity of his efforts in the legislature, and later the exertion of his personal influence, to secure the legal abolition of the entire system. Closely allied to his desire to abolish slavery, and derived from the same belief in the intrinsic worth of every man, was his desire to abolish the legal right of primogeniture and the entailing of estates. This, unlike the abolition of slavery, he was able to enact into law. Both efforts had the same foundation, the desire to do away with any artificial restrictions on the development of each individual to his fullest capacity, and the desire to make opportunities equal as far as artifice permitted and nature did not reject.

The second belief he derived from that in the innate capacity of man was a belief in the value of education and the need of a comprehensive system of common schools, maintained at the expense of the community, giving to every child, rich and poor, sufficient education to make him capable of exercising rightly his duties as a citizen, and culminating for those worthy of it

INTRODUCTION

in the higher education in a state university. His father had had but little schooling and was a self-educated man. Jefferson himself, if not the profoundest thinker of his age and country, was probably its most broadly cultivated man. A fair musician, an unusually good architect, interested in all the scientific thought of the day, a wide reader in French, English, and classical literatures, a deep student of government, and a man who had had peculiar opportunities for studying governments and revolutionary movements on two continents, he never lost his belief in the value and influence of education. The conditions of his day were comparatively simple, but in his insistence on man's innate right-mindedness and capacity for self-government, and the need, on the one hand, for doing away with any hampering economic conditions then existing, and on the other, the fostering of man's capacities by education, he clearly showed the trend of his thought.

Following the argument, namely: that man is innately capable of self-government under the right conditions; that, for the great majority of Americans at that time, conditions were right; and that they should be made better for all by the abolition of slavery, entail, and other hindrances, and the educating of all classes, he went on logically to other conclusions. Man should enjoy as perfect liberty, both religious and political, as he was capable of, and in America, Jefferson believed, he was capable of an almost unlimited amount of each. In accordance with this belief, Jefferson struggled for complete religious toleration in his own state and secured the passage of the broadest law of any of the United States at the time. As for political liberty, he always fought for as great a measure as was compatible with men living in civilized social contacts, retaining unlimited faith, undimmed to the end, in the use which his fellow citizens would make of it.

From all these premises, so naturally growing out of one another, he derived his general ideas on the nature of government. In his First Inaugural he summed up the function of government, briefly, as the prevention of men from injuring one another, and although he elaborated this to include a number of functions in practice, he always believed that there should be as little government as possible. He believed men to be capable of regulating their own concerns wisely and honestly, and that government should attempt to accomplish for them only certain acts in their corporate capacity, which, as scattered and noncoöperating individuals, they could not accomplish for themselves. He believed a certain minimum activity of government thus to be necessary, but that did not invalidate in his opinion the fact that government was an evil, though a necessary one, and that its powers and activities should always be jealously kept down to the very lowest point possible, so as to infringe as little as might be on the complete independence and liberty of the free-willing and acting individual.

Considering government thus to be not something imposed on mankind by a select minority of the wise and good for the benefit of the less fit, capable, and honest multitude, but something which that multitude itself should manage solely for its own benefit and by itself, he believed that such government as there was should always be kept as closely under the control of the multitude as was possible. This was the reason for many of his doctrines enounced in detail, such as his desire to entrust as little power as possible to the Federal government and not only keep as much as possible in the hands of the state governments but to carry the

INTRODUCTION

downward gradation still further. Opposed as he was to much in the New England system of political thought, he was always a great admirer of the town government of that section. He would have the smallest local political unit administer all the governmental functions it was capable of. Only such functions as it could not perform should, as a necessary evil, be passed to the next higher unit, and so on. As he saw it, there was almost nothing of which the highest local units, the states, were not capable of attending to except foreign policy and a very few of the most general concerns of the nation as united. This same idea, of keeping the government always as close to the people as possible, was at the bottom of his belief in short terms of office, especially of his strong belief, expressed again and again throughout life, that the President should not be eligible for more than one reëlection. He himself declined to run for a third term and he felt that the possibility some day of an ambitious man trying to do so was one of the greatest dangers to be feared for the liberties of the country. It was this belief, again, that was at the root of another secondary belief, frequently elaborated in his letters. This was that no government had the right to incur debts for a longer period than one generation, and that each generation should pay its way completely as it went, as much in its corporate as in its individual life. In fact he expanded this doctrine rather fantastically, so as to suggest that even the Constitution should be revised every twenty years, or whatever might be considered the life of a generation, so as not to infringe on the liberties of the next.

Jefferson's whole system of political thought, with its many practical applications, becomes clear if we keep the above fundamental beliefs of his in mind. They were beliefs in which he never wavered in spite of all he had himself seen of the excesses and stupidities to which man in the mass might commit himself, both in France and elsewhere. Mere revolution and even a certain amount of violence did not disturb his philosophy. He went so far as to say that perhaps a bit of revolution every twenty years or so was desirable, as indicating vitality of liberty in the body politic.

Although Jefferson stood for democracy, he himself was an aristocrat. He might preach the gospel of the rights of the common man and express his disdain, in a democracy, for titles and many of the social conventions, but he was

INTRODUCTION

far from the nature of the common man himself. His own home at Monticello, which, as well as the buildings of the University of Virginia, was designed by him, shows an exquisitely refined taste. His letters reveal a man not only of intellectual ability but of literary cultivation and trained appreciation. In his open-handed hospitality, his unfailing courtesy, and ungrudging generosity to all who came or wrote to him after he became famous, and in his incurring of heavy debts for what he considered the higher purposes of his own life, there was nothing of the plebeian or of the calculating prudence of the cautious middle class. Perhaps the aristocratic quality in him came out most strongly in his utter disdain of what the people had to say of him, and no other man of his day was more bitterly assailed, not only in press but in pulpit. He would condescend neither to retaliate nor to explain.

Some of the undeserved obloquy thrown upon him by clergymen who should have known better has clung to him to this day, and the extracts here given of his thoughts on religion may come as a surprise to many. Not long ago, a man who claims to be intelligent and well-read insisted to me that Jefferson was an atheist. That was

INTRODUCTION

the accusation hurled at him constantly through
life from the New England pulpits, but he always simply said that his religion was a matter
between himself and God, and refused to throw
back mud at the scurrilous ministers who
prostituted their high office. In reality, religion — not theology — occupied much of his
thoughts, even during the busy years of the
presidency.

In the last section I have gathered together
a few scattered thoughts on the conduct of life.
Most of these are taken from letters written to
young people, of whom he was always fond,
and were penned during his maturer years.

If Jefferson could return to-day to see the
country for which he gave the best efforts of
his entire life, it would be impossible to tell
what he might say. He would find conditions
so altered that his own opinions on many topics
might have to be altered also. He himself
explicitly warned us not to live in the past nor to
guide ourselves too much by the opinions of
"the fathers." Keenly interested in science
and in every new invention, he would marvel
at the progress made in applied knowledge,
but his mind was direct and his philosophy
simple, and it is not likely that he would long

be dazzled by the material triumphs of his countrymen. He would press forward at once to inquire into the fundamental problems of government and human nature.

He would find that great progress had been made in removing the handicaps from which the less fortunate had suffered. Slavery he would find to his joy had been abolished, though he would properly realize at once the intense gravity of the race problem which has been left in its place. He would also see that one of the things he most feared had come to pass and, so far from being an agricultural country, more than one half of the people were now living in cities, the very condition which he feared might spell the ruin of popular government and make men unfit to govern themselves. He would also see that free public education had been carried to a height almost undreamed of by him, yet he would realize that its results have been disappointing. He would observe that schools and colleges may make people literate but cannot make them learned or wise, and that the mass of the people whom he would have educated with such care for the purpose of making them wise citizens preferred reams of the headline-tabloid press and sensational movies to any five minutes of genuine consecutive thought. He would find the functions of the central government swollen to a degree that he never dreamed of, and, on the other hand, the governments in many cases nearest to the people, municipal and state, the most full of rottenness. He would find that some of the liberties for which he fought hardest and which he believed the common man most cared for, liberty of speech and liberty of the press, for example, had been discarded by them to a great extent without a thought or regret on the part of most of them. He would find a world in which his doctrine of democracy was on trial in public opinion as it had scarcely been before since his own generation. What would he say?

It is impossible to tell, but that he would go over to the side of Hamilton is unlikely. The difference between the two men was a matter of temperament, to give the whole obscure complex of reactions some name. It may have been due, according to modern biographic jargon, to blood pressure, glands, or what you will, but it was the difference between the man who instinctively fears and him who instinctively trusts. Jefferson's faith in man surmounted all he saw in the French Revolution.

INTRODUCTION

It surmounted Shays's Rebellion. It surmounted
all that he, an aristocrat to his finger tips, whatever his origin, well knew of the nature of that
common man with whom he was so well
acquainted. The balance sheet to-day of gains
and losses is by no means clear. Perhaps no
form of government can be permanent, and
man is doomed to whirl forever down eternal
cycles of change. No one can yet say whether
democracy is going to fail or succeed. The
question is still as open to dispute as it was
in 1789. The problem which Hamilton and
Jefferson fought over — can the common man
be trusted to govern himself and others? — is
still a living one. With all its increased com-
plexity, it is the same old problem, and it is
probable that, were they both alive to-day,
Hamilton and Jefferson would be found fighting
on the same sides on which they fought a
hundred and more years ago.

If so, as all Jefferson's political philosophy
springs, as we have tried very briefly to show,
from his belief in the ability and right-willing
of the common man, the main outlines of his
attitude to-day would not be difficult to define.
His opinions might be altered on details, but
his faith in the common man would probably

INTRODUCTION

remain unaltered, and the same corollaries would flow from the fundamental fact in his thinking as flowed before. These would be: to keep government as close to the people as possible; to limit its functions as much as possible; to knock off as many shackles on the free development of the individual as possible; to give him as much and as *fit* education as possible; and to preserve to him as much freedom of thought, speech, action, taste, and habit as possible; to limit government debt and expenditure as much as possible; to re-arouse in the individual a sense of independence and self-reliance as much as possible; and to free intercourse with foreign nations as much as possible. And that "as much as possible" would be an extent far beyond what would be considered feasible by the cautious and conservative. We cannot, of course, say, but a careful study of the man's whole writings, of his opinions on all the problems of his own day, and of his reactions to all opposing conditions which might have been expected to alter — if anything would — those opinions, indicates that something like the above would be the platform on which Jefferson would appeal to the people to-day.

JAMES TRUSLOW ADAMS

[xx]

CHRONOLOGY

1743 April 2, born at Shadwell, Albemarle County, Virginia.
1757 His father, Peter Jefferson, died.
1767 Admitted to the bar in Virginia.
1769 Became member of the House of Burgesses.
1772 January 1, married Mrs. Martha Skelton.
Moved to Monticello.
1774 Wrote draft of instructions for Virginia delegates to Congress.
1775 Member of the Virginia Convention.
Member of the Continental Congress.
1776 Wrote Declaration of Independence.
Resigned from Congress.
Reëlected to the Virginia legislature.
1776/7 On committee to revise laws and constitution of Virginia.
1779 Elected Governor of Virginia.
1782 Wife died.
1783 Elected to Congress.
1784/9 In France as Minister Plenipotentiary.
1789 Appointed Secretary of State.
1794 Resigned from the Cabinet.
1796 Elected Vice President of the United States.
1798 Wrote the Kentucky Resolutions.
1800 Elected President of the United States.
1804 Reëlected President.
1809 Refused renomination and retired to Monticello.
1826 July 4, died.

NOTE

UNLESS specifically noted otherwise, the cita-
tions for all the selections are to the volumes and
page numbers of the edition of Jefferson's
writings edited by Paul Leicester Ford, in ten
volumes, published by G. P. Putnam's Sons,
1892.

In quoting, I have in no case changed the
text in any particular except occasionally to
expand a contraction, such as *government* for
govt., *them* for *ym*, etc.

J. T. A.

CONTENTS

POLITICAL PRINCIPLES AND
PRACTICE

POLITICAL PRINCIPLES AND PRACTICE

We hold these truths to be self-evident that all men are created equal; that they are endowed by their creator with inherent & inalienable rights, that among these are life, liberty, and the pursuit of happiness; that to secure these rights governments are instituted among men deriving their just powers from the consent of the governed; that whenever any form of government becomes destructive of these ends, it is the right of the people to alter or to abolish it, and to institute new government, laying its foundation on such principles and organizing its powers in such form, as to them shall seem most likely to effect their happiness. Prudence indeed will dictate that governments long established should not be changed for light and transient causes: and accordingly all experience hath shown that mankind are more disposed to suffer while evils are sufferable, than to right themselves by abolishing the forms to which

[3]

they are accustomed. But when a long train of abuses and usurpations begun at a distinguished period and pursuing invariably the same object, evinces a design to reduce them under absolute despotism, it is their right, it is their duty, to throw off such government and to provide new guards for their future security. — *Declaration of Independence.* Vol. II, pp. 43-45. [This is from one of the copies in Jefferson's own handwriting, representing the form in which it was transmitted from the committee to Congress. — Ed.]

THE SUM OF GOOD GOVERNMENT

With all these blessings, what more is necessary to make us a happy and a prosperous people? Still one thing more, fellow citizens, a wise & frugal government, which shall restrain men from injuring one another, shall leave them otherwise free to regulate their own pursuits of industry & improvement, and shall not take from the mouth of labor the bread it has earned. This is the sum of good government, & this is necessary to close the circle of our felicities. — *First Inaugural Address*, March 4, 1801. Vol. VIII, p. 4.

JEFFERSONIAN PRINCIPLES

THE ESSENTIAL PRINCIPLES OF THE AMERICAN GOVERNMENT

It is proper you should understand what I deem the essential principles of this government and consequently those which ought to shape its administration.

I will compress them in the narrowest compass they will bear, stating the general principle, but not all it's limitations.

Equal and exact justice to all men, of whatever state or persuasion, religious or political:

Peace, commerce, and honest friendship with all nations, entangling alliances with none:

The support of the State governments in all their rights, as the most competent administrations for our domestic concerns, and the surest bulwarks against anti republican tendencies:

The preservation of the General government, in it's whole constitutional vigor, as the sheet anchor of our peace at home, and safety abroad.

A jealous care of the right of election by the people, a mild and sage corrective of abuses, which are lopped by the sword of revolution, where peaceable remedies are unprovided.

Absolute acquiescence in the decisions of the Majority the vital principle of republics, from which is no appeal but to force, the vital principle and immediate part of despotism.

A well disciplined militia, our best reliance in peace, and for the first moments of war, till regulars may relieve them: The Supremacy of the Civil over the Military authority:

Economy in public expense, that labor may be lightly burthened:

The honest paiment of our debts and sacred preservation of the public faith:

Encouragement of Agriculture, and of Commerce as it's handmaid:

The diffusion of information, and arraignment of all abuses at the bar of the public reason:

Freedom of Religion, freedom of the press, and freedom of Person under the protection of the Habeas Corpus: And trial by juries, impartially selected. — *First Inaugural*, 1801. Vol. VIII, pp. 4–5.

ON HIS POLITICAL BELIEFS

I am for preserving to the States the powers not yielded by them to the Union, & to the legislature of the Union it's constitutional share in the division of powers; and I am not for transferring all the powers of the States to the general government, & all those of that government to the Executive branch. I am for a government rigorously frugal & simple, applying all the possible savings of the public revenue to the discharge of the national debt; and not for a multiplication of officers & salaries merely to make partisans, & for increasing, by every device, the public debt, on the principle of it's being a public blessing. I am for relying, for internal defence, on our militia solely, till actual invasion, and for such a naval force only as may protect our coasts and harbors from such depredations as we have experienced; and not for a standing army in time of peace, which may overawe the public sentiment; nor for a navy, which, by it's own expenses and the eternal wars in which it will implicate us, will grind us with public burthens, & sink us under them. I am for free commerce with all nations; political connection with none; & little or no diplomatic establishment. And I am not for linking ourselves by new treaties with the quarrels of Europe; entering that field of slaughter to preserve their balance, or joining in the confederacy of kings to war against the principles of liberty. I am for freedom of religion, & against all maneuvres to bring about a legal ascendancy of one sect over another: for freedom of the press & against all violations of the constitution to silence by force & not by reason the complaints or criticism, just or unjust, of our citizens against the conduct of their agents. And I am for encouraging the progress of science in all it's branches; and not for raising a hue and cry against the sacred name of philosophy; for awing the human mind by stories of raw-head & bloody bones to a distrust of its own vision, & to repose implicitly on that of others; to go backwards instead of forwards to look for improvement; to believe that government, religion, morality, & every other science were in the highest perfection in ages of the darkest ignorance, and that nothing can ever be devised more perfect than what was established by our forefathers. To these I will add, that I was a sincere well-wisher to the success of the French revolution, and still wish it may end in the establishment of a free & well-ordered republic; but I have not been insensible under the atrocious depredations they have committed on our commerce. The first object of my heart is my own country. In that is embarked my family, my fortune, & my own existence. I have not one farthing of interest, nor one fibre of attachment out of it, nor a single motive of preference of any one nation to another, but in proportion as they are more or less friendly to us. — *Letter to Elbridge Gerry*, January 26, 1799.   Vol. VII, pp. 328–329.

On the People as the Source of Power

In every government on earth is some trace of human weakness, some germ of corruption and degeneracy, which cunning will discover, and wickedness insensibly open, cultivate and improve.   Every government degenerates when trusted to the rulers of the people alone.   The people themselves therefore are its only safe depositories.   And to render them safe, their minds must be improved to a certain degree. This indeed is not all that is necessary, though it be essentially necessary.   An amendment of our constitution must here come in aid of public education.   The influence over government must be shared among all the people.   If every individual which composes their mass partici- pates of the ultimate authority, the government will be safe; because the corrupting the whole mass will exceed any private resources of wealth; and public ones cannot be provided but by levies on the people.   In this case every man would have to pay his own price. . . .   It has been thought that corruption is restrained by confining the right of suffrage to a few of the wealthier of the people: but it would be more effectually restrained by an extension of that right to such numbers as would bid defiance to the means of corruption. — *Notes on Virginia.* Vol. III, pp. 254–255.

We think in America that it is necessary to introduce the people into every department of government as far as they are capable of exercising it; and that this is the only way to ensure a long continued & honest administration of it's powers. 1. They are not qualified to exercise themselves the Executive department; but they are qualified to name the person who shall exercise it. With us therefore they chuse this office every 4. years. 2. They are not qualified to Legislate. With us therefore they only chuse the legislators. 3. They are not qualified to *Judge* questions of *law;* but they are very capable of judging questions of *fact.* In the form of juries therefore they determine all matters of fact, leaving to the permanent judges to decide the law resulting from those facts. But we all know, that permanent judges acquire an *Esprit de corps,* that being known they are liable to be tempted by bribery, that they are misled by favor, by relationship, by a spirit of party, by a devotion to the Executive or Legislative; that it is better to leave a cause to the decision of cross & pile, than to that of a judge biased to one side; and that the opinion of 12. honest jurymen gives still a better hope of right, than cross & pile does. It is left therefore to the juries, if they think the permanent judges are under any biass whatever in any cause, to take on themselves to judge the law as well as the fact. They never exercise this power but when they suspect partiality in the judges, and by the exercise of this power they have been the firmest bulwarks of English liberty. Were I called upon to decide whether the people had best be omitted in the Legislative or Judiciary department, I would say it is better to leave them out of the Legislature. The execution of the laws is more important than the making them. However it is best to have the people in all the three departments where that is possible. — *Letter to the Abbé Arnond*, July 19, 1789. Vol. V, pp. 103–104.

On Our Natural Aristocracy

I agree with you that there is a natural aristocracy among men. The grounds of this

[11]

are virtue and talents.   Formerly, bodily powers
gave place among the aristoi.   But since the
invention of gunpowder has armed the weak as
well as the strong with missile death, bodily
strength, like beauty, good humor, politeness
and other accomplishments, has become but
an auxiliary ground for distinction.   There is
also an artificial aristocracy, founded on wealth
and birth, without either virtue or talents; for
with these it would belong to the first class.
The natural aristocracy I consider as the most
precious gift of nature, for the instruction, the
trusts, and government of society.   And indeed,
it would have been inconsistent in creation to
have formed man for the social state, and not
to have provided virtue and wisdom enough
to manage the concerns of the society.   May
we not even say, that that form of government
is the best, which provides the most effectually
for a pure selection of these natural aristoi into
the offices of government?   The artificial aristocracy is a mischievous ingredient in government, and provision should be made to prevent
its ascendency.   On the question, what is the
best provision, you and I differ; but we differ
as rational friends, using the free exercise of our
own reason, and mutually indulging its errors.

JEFFERSONIAN PRINCIPLES

You think it best to put the pseudo-aristoi into a separate chamber of legislation, where they may be hindered from doing mischief by their co-ordinate branches, and where, also, they may be a protection to wealth against the Agrarian and plundering enterprises of the majority of the people. I think that to give them power in order to prevent them from doing mischief, is arming them for it, and increasing instead of remedying the evil. For if the co-ordinate branches can arrest their action, so may they that of the co-ordinates. Mischief can be done negatively as well as positively. Of this, a cabal in the Senate of the United States has furnished many proofs. Nor do I believe them necessary to protect the wealthy; because enough of these will find their way into every branch of the legislation, to protect themselves. From fifteen to twenty legislatures of our own, in action for thirty years past, have proved that no fears of an equalization of property are to be apprehended from them. I think the best remedy is exactly that provided by all our constitutions, to leave to the citizens the free election and separation of the aristoi from the pseudo-aristoi, of the wheat from the chaff. In general they will elect the really good and wise. In some instances, wealth may corrupt, and birth blind them; but not in sufficient degree to endanger the society. . . .

With respect to aristocracy, we should further consider, that before the establishment of the American States, nothing was known to history but the man of the old world, crowded within limits either small or overcharged, and steeped in the vices which that situation generates. A government adapted to such men would be one thing; but a very different one, that for the man of these States. Here every one may have land to labor for himself, if he chooses; or, preferring the exercise of any other industry, may exact from it such compensation as not only to afford a comfortable subsistence, but wherewith to provide for a cessation from labor in old age. Every one, by his property, or by his satisfactory situation, is interested in the support of law and order. And such men may safely and advantageously reserve to themselves a wholesome control over their public affairs, and a degree of freedom, which, in the hands of the *canaille* of the cities of Europe, would be instantly perverted to the demolition and destruction of everything public and private. — *Letter to John Adams*, October 28, 1814.   Vol. IX, pp. 425–428.

On Natural and Artificial Aristocracies

In the earlier times of the colony when lands were to be obtained for little or nothing, some provident individuals procured large grants, and, desirous of founding great families for themselves, settled them on their descendants in fee-tail.   The transmission of this property from generation to generation in the same name raised up a distinct set of families who, being privileged by law in the perpetuation of their wealth were thus formed into a Patrician order, distinguished by the splendor and luxury of their establishments. . . .   To annul this privilege, and instead of an aristocracy of wealth, of more harm and danger, than benefit to society, to make an opening for the aristocracy of virtue and talent, which nature has wisely provided for the direction of the interests of society, & scattered with equal hand through all its conditions, was deemed essential to a well ordered republic. — *Autobiography*.   Vol. I, p. 49.   [On October 12, 1776, Jefferson introduced a bill into the Virginia legislature, subsequently passed, declaring that tenants in tail should thereafter hold their lands in fee simple. —Ed.]

On Primogeniture

As the law of Descents, & the criminal law fell of course within my portion, I wished the committee to settle the leading principles of these, as a guide for me in framing them. And with respect to the first I proposed to abolish the law of primogeniture, and to make real estate descendible in parcenary to the next of kin, as personal property is by the statute of distribution. Mr. Pendleton wished to preserve the right of primogeniture, but seeing at once that that could not prevail, he proposed we should adopt the Hebrew principle, and give a double portion to the elder son. I observed that if the eldest son could eat twice as much, or do double work, it might be a natural evidence of his right to a double portion; but being on a par in his powers & wants, with his brothers and sisters, he should be on a par also in the partition of the patrimony, and such was the decision of the other members.

On the subject of the Criminal Law, all were agreed that the punishment of death should be abolished, except for treason and murder; and that, for other felonies should be substituted hard labor in the public works, and in some cases, the Lex talionis. How this last revolting principle came to obtain our approbation, I do not remember. — *Autobiography*. Vol. I, pp. 59–60. [In 1779 Jefferson was a member of the legislative committee appointed to revise the state laws in Virginia. — Ed.]

On the Will of the Nation

We surely cannot deny to any nation that right where on our own government is founded, that every one may govern itself under whatever forms it pleases, and change these forms at its own will, and that it may transact it's business with foreign nations through whatever organ it thinks proper, whether King, convention, assembly, committee, President, or whatever else it may chuse. The will of the nation is the only thing essential to be regarded. — *Letter to the U. S. Minister to France*, December 30, 1792. Vol. VI, p. 149.

On Majority Rule

It is my principle that the will of the majority should always prevail. If they approve the

JEFFERSONIAN PRINCIPLES

proposed Convention in all it's parts, I shall concur in it chearfully, in hopes that they will amend it whenever they shall find it work wrong. I think our governments will remain virtuous for many centuries; as long as they are chiefly agricultural; and this will be as long as there shall be vacant lands in any part of America. When they get piled upon one another in large cities, as in Europe, they will become corrupt as in Europe. Above all things I hope the education of the common people will be attended to; convinced that on their good sense we may rely with the most security for the preservation of a due degree of liberty. — *Letter to James Madison*, December 20, 1787. Vol. IV, pp. 479–480.

On Majorities and Morality

I believe with you that morality, compassion, generosity, are innate elements of the human constitution; that there exists a right independent of force; that a right to property is founded in our natural wants, in the means with which we are endowed to satisfy these wants, and the right to what we acquire by those means without violating the similar rights of other sensible beings; that no one has a right

JEFFERSONIAN PRINCIPLES

to obstruct another, exercising his faculties
innocently for the relief of sensibilities made a
part of his nature; that justice is the fundamental law of society; that the majority, oppressing
an individual, is guilty of a crime, abuses its
strength, and by acting on the law of the
strongest breaks up the foundations of society;
that action by the citizens in person, in affairs
within their reach and competence, and in all
others by representatives, chosen immediately,
and removable by themselves, constitutes the
essence of a republic. . . . — *Letter to P. S.
DuPont de Nemours*, April 24, 1816. Vol. X,
p. 24.

On Majorities and Minorities

During the contest of opinion through which
we have passed, the animation of discussions
and of exertions, has sometimes worn an aspect
which might impose on strangers unused to
think freely, and to speak and to write what they
think.

But this being now decided by the voice of
the nation, enounced according to the rules of
the constitution, all will of course arrange
themselves under the will of the law, and unite
in common efforts for the common good. All

too will bear in mind the sacred principle that tho the will of the Majority is in all cases to prevail, that will, to be rightful, must be reasonable: that the Minority possess their equal rights, which equal laws must protect, and to violate would be oppression. — *First Inaugural*, 1801.   Vol. VIII, p. 2.

On the Place of Fear in Government

If our government ever fails, it will be from this weakness.   No government can be maintained without the principle of fear as well as of duty.   Good men will obey the last, but bad ones the former only. — *Letter to John Wayles Eppes*, September 9, 1814.   Vol. IX, p. 484.

On the Limits of Legislative Power

Our legislators are not sufficiently apprized of the rightful limits of their power; that their true office is to declare and enforce only our natural rights and duties, and to take none of them from us.   No man has a natural right to commit aggression on the equal rights of another; and this is all from which the laws ought to restrain him; every man is under the natural duty of contributing to the necessities of the society; and this is all the laws should enforce on him; and, no man having a natural right to be the judge between himself and another, it is his natural duty to submit to the umpirage of an impartial third. When the laws have declared and enforced all this, they have fulfilled their functions, and the idea is quite unfounded, that on entering into society we give up any natural right. — *Letter to Francis W. Gilmer*, June 7, 1816. Vol. X, p. 32.

On Certain Rights

There are rights which it is useless to surrender to the government, and which governments have yet always been fond to invade. These are the rights of thinking, and publishing our thoughts by speaking or writing; the right of free commerce; the right of personal freedom. There are instruments for administering the government, so peculiarly trustworthy, that we should never leave the legislature at liberty to change them. The new constitution has secured these in the executive & legislative departments; but not in the judiciary. It should have established trials by the people themselves, that is to say by jury. There are instruments so dangerous to the rights of the nation, and which place them so totally at the mercy of their governors, that those governors, whether legislative or executive, should be restrained from keeping such instruments on foot, but in well-defined cases. Such an instrument is a standing army. — *Letter to David Humphreys*, March 18, 1789. Vol. V, pp. 89–90.

On the Meaning of "Republic"

On this view of the import of the term *republic*, instead of saying, as has been said, "that it may mean anything or nothing," we may say with truth and meaning, that governments are more or less republican as they have more or less of the element of popular election and control in their composition; and believing, as I do, that the mass of the citizens is the safest depositary of their own rights, and especially, that the evils flowing from the duperies of the people, are less injurious than those from the egoism of their agents, I am a friend to that composition of government which has in it the most of this ingredient. And I sincerely believe, with you, that banking establishments are more dangerous than standing armies; and that the principle of spending money to be paid by posterity, under the name of funding, is but swindling futurity on a large scale. — *Letter to John Taylor*, May 28, 1816. Vol. X, p. 31.

On the Constitution

The three great questions of amendment [to the Federal Constitution] now before you, will give the measure of their strength. I mean, 1st, the limitation of the term of presidential service; 2d, the placing the choice of president effectually in the hands of the people; 3d, the giving to Congress the power of internal improvement, on condition that each State's federal proportion of the monies so expended, shall be employed within the State. . . . The real friends of the constitution in its federal form, if they wish it to be immortal, should be attentive, by amendments, to make it keep pace with the advance of the age in science and experience. . . . If I can see these three great amendments prevail, I shall consider it as a renewed extension of the term of our lease, shall live in more confidence, and die in more hope. — *Letter to Robert J. Garnett*, February 14, 1824. Vol. X, p. 295.

JEFFERSONIAN PRINCIPLES

On a Strict Interpretation of the Constitution

I consider the foundation of the Constitution as laid on this ground: That "all powers not delegated to the United States, by the Constitution, nor prohibited by it to the States, are reserved to the States or to the people." [XIIth amendment]. To take a single step beyond the boundaries thus specifically drawn around the powers of Congress, is to take possession of a boundless field of power, no longer susceptible of any definition. The incorporation of a bank, and the powers assumed by this bill, have not, in my opinion, been delegated to the United States, by the Constitution. They are not among the powers specially enumerated. . . . Nor are they within either of the general phrases, which are the two following: — "To lay taxes to provide for the general welfare of the United States. . . . To make all laws necessary and proper for the carrying into execution of the enumerated powers. . . ." They can all be carried into execution without a bank. . . . It has been urged that a bank will give great facility or convenience in the collection of taxes. Suppose this were true : yet the Constitution allows only the means which are "*necessary*," not those which are merely "convenient" for effecting the enumerated powers. If such a latitude of construction be allowed to this phrase as to give any non-enumerated power, it will go to every one, for there is not one which ingenuity may not torture into a *convenience* in some instance *or other*, to *some one* of so long a list of enumerated powers. It would swallow up all the delegated powers, and reduce the whole to one power, as before observed. Therefore it was that the Constitution restrained them to the *necessary* means, that is to say, to those means without which the grant of power would be nugatory. . . . Can it be thought that the Constitution intended that for a shade or two of *convenience*, more or less, Congress should be authorised to break down the most ancient and fundamental laws of the several States; such as those against Mortmain, the laws of Alienage, the rules of descent, the acts of distribution, the laws of escheat and forfeiture, the laws of monopoly ? Nothing but a necessity invincible by any other means, can justify such a prostitution of laws, which constitute the pillars of our whole system of jurisprudence. Will Congress be too straight-laced to carry the constitution into honest effect, unless they may pass over the foundation-laws of the State government for the slightest convenience of theirs? The negative of the President is the shield provided by the constitution to protect against the invasions of the legislature: 1. The right of the Executive. 2. Of the Judiciary. 3. Of the States and State legislatures. The present is the case of a right remaining exclusively with the States, and consequently one of those intended by the Constitution to be placed under its protection. It must be added, however, that unless the President's mind on a view of everything which is urged for and against this bill, is tolerably clear that it is unauthorised by the Constitution; if the pro and con hang so even as to balance his judgment, a just respect for the wisdom of the legislature would naturally decide the balance in favor of their opinion. It is chiefly for cases where they are clearly misled by error, ambition, or interest, that the Constitution has placed a check in the negative of the President. — *Opinion on the Constitutionality of a National Bank*, February 15, 1791. Vol. V, pp. 285–289.

JEFFERSONIAN PRINCIPLES

On Constitutional Revision

Some men look at constitutions with sanctimonious reverence, and deem them like the arc of the covenant, too sacred to be touched. They ascribe to the men of the preceding age a wisdom more than human, and suppose what they did to be beyond amendment. I knew that age well; I belonged to it, and labored with it. It deserved well of its country. It was very like the present, but without the experience of the present; and forty years of experience in government is worth a century of book-reading; and this they would say themselves, were they to rise from the dead. I am certainly not an advocate for frequent and untried changes in laws and constitutions. I think moderate imperfections had better be borne with; because, when once known, we accomodate ourselves to them, and find practical means of correcting ther ill effects. But I know also, that laws and institutions must go hand in hand with the progress of the human mind. As that becomes more developed, more enlightened, as new discoveries are made, new truths disclosed, and manners and opinions change with the change of circumstances, institutions must advance also, and keep pace with the times. We might as well require a man to wear still the coat which fitted him when a boy, as civilized society to remain ever under the regimen of their barbarous ancestors. . . . Let us, as our sister States have done, avail ourselves of our reason and experience, to correct the crude essays of our first and unexperienced, although wise, virtuous, and well, meaning councils. And, lastly, let us provide in our constitution [that of Virginia] for its revision at stated periods. What these periods should be, nature herself indicates. . . . [Every generation of nineteen years.] If this avenue [of legal revision] be shut to the call of sufferance, it will make itself heard through that of force, and we shall go on, as other nations are doing, in the endless circle of oppression, rebellion, reformation; and oppression, rebellion, reformation, again; and so on forever. — *Letter to Samuel Kercheval,* July 12, 1816. Vol. X, pp. 42–43.

On Revising the Virginia State Constitution

I shall hazard my own ideas to you as hastily as my business obliges me. I wish to preserve the line drawn by the federal constitution

between the general & particular governments
as it stands at present, and to take every
prudent means of preventing either from step-
ping over it. Tho' the experiment has not yet
had a long enough course to shew us from
which quarter encroachments are most to be
feared, yet it is easy to foresee from the nature
of things that the encroachments of the state
governments will tend to an excess of liberty
which will correct itself (as in the late instance)
while those of the general government will tend
to monarchy, which will fortify itself from day
to day, instead of working its own cure, as all
experience shews. I would rather be exposed
to the inconveniencies attending too much
liberty than those attending too small a degree
of it. Then it is important to strengthen the
state governments: and as this cannot be done
by any change in the federal constitution, (for
the preservation of that is all we need contend
for,) it must be done by the states themselves,
erecting such barriers at the constitutional line
as cannot be surmounted either by themselves
or by the general government. The only bar-
rier in their power is a wise government. A
weak one will lose ground in every contest. To
obtain a wise & an able government, I consider

the following changes as important. Render the legislature a desirable station by lessening the number of representatives (say to 100) and lengthening somewhat their term, and proportion them equally among the electors: adopt also a better mode of appointing Senators. Render the Executive a more desirable post to men of abilities by making it more independent of the legislature. To wit, let him be chosen by other electors, for a longer time, and ineligible for ever after. Responsibility is a tremendous engine in a free government. Let him feel the whole weight of it then by taking away the shelter of his executive council. Experience both ways has already established the superiority of this measure. Render the Judiciary respectable by every possible means, to wit, firm tenure in office, competent salaries, and reduction of their numbers. Men of high learning and abilities are few in every country; — by taking in those who are not so, the able part of the body have their hands tied by the unable. This branch of the government will have the weight of the conflict on their hands, because they will be the last appeal of reason. — *Letter to Archibald Stuart*, December 23, 1791. Vol. V, pp. 409–410.

JEFFERSONIAN PRINCIPLES

The true foundation of republican government is the equal right of every citizen, in his person and property, and in their management. Try by this, as a tally, every provision of our constitution, and see if it hangs directly on the will of the people. Reduce your legislature to a convenient number for full, but orderly discussion. Let every man who fights or pays, exercise his just and equal rights in their election. Submit them to approbation or rejection at short intervals. Let the executive be chosen in the same way, and for the same term, by those whose agent he is to be; and leave no screen of a council behind which to skulk from responsibility. It has been thought that the people are not competent electors of judges *learned in the law*. But I do not know that this is true, and, if doubtful, we should follow principle. In this, as in many other elections, they would be guided by reputation, which would not err oftener, perhaps, than the present mode of appointment. In one State of the Union, at least, it has long been tried, and with the most satisfactory success. . . .

Nomination to office is an executive function. To give it to the legislature, as we do, is a violation of the principle of the separation of powers. It swerves the members from correctness, by temptations to intrigue for office themselves, and to a corrupt barter of votes; and destroys responsibility by dividing it among a multitude. . . . — *Letter to Samuel Kercheval,* July 12, 1816. Vol. X, pp. 39–40.

On the Division of Governmental Powers

It is not by the consolidation, or concentration of powers, but by their distribution, that good government is effected. Were not this great country already divided into states, that division must be made, that each might do for itself what concerns itself directly, and what it can so much better do than a distant authority. Every state again is divided into counties, each to take care of what lies within it's local bounds; each county again into townships or wards, to manage minuter details; and every ward into farms, to be governed each by it's individual proprietor. Were we directed from Washington when to sow, & when to reap, we should soon want bread. It is by this partition of cares, descending in gradation from general to particular, that the mass of human affairs may be best managed for the good and prosperity of all. — *Autobiography*. Vol. I, p. 113.

I think it very material to separate in the hands of Congress the Executive & Legislative powers, as the Judiciary already are in some degree. This I hope will be done. The want of it has been a source of more evil than we have experienced from any other cause. Nothing is so embarrassing nor so mischievous in a great assembly as the details of execution. The smallest trifle of that kind occupies as long as the most important act of legislation, & takes place of everything else. Let any man recollect, or look over, the files of Congress, he will observe the most important propositions hanging over from week to week & month to month, till the occasions have past them, & the thing is never done. I have ever viewed the executive details as the greatest cause of evil to us, because they in fact place us as if we had no federal head, by diverting the attention of that head from great to small objects; and should this division of power not be recommended by the Convention, it is my opinion Congress should make it itself by establishing an Executive committee. — *Letter to Edward*

JEFFERSONIAN PRINCIPLES

Carrington, August 4, 1787.   Vol. IV, pp. 424–425.

On the Powers of the Federal Government

Resolved, That the several States composing the United States of America, are not united on the principle of unlimited submission to their general government; but that, by a compact under the style and title of a Constitution for the United States, and of amendments thereto, they constituted a general government for special purposes, — delegated to that government certain definite powers, reserving, each State to itself, the residuary mass of right to their own self-government; and that whensoever the general government assumes undelegated powers, its acts are unauthoritative, void, and of no force: that to this compact each State acceded as a State, and is an integral party, its co-States forming, as to itself, the other party: that the government created by this compact was not made the exclusive or final judge of the extent of the powers delegated to itself; since that would have made its discretion, and not the Constitution, the measure of its powers; but that, as in all other cases of compact among powers having no common judge, each party has an equal right to judge for itself, as well of infractions as of the mode and measure of redress.

Resolved, That the Constitution of the United States having delegated to Congress a power to punish treason, counterfeiting the securities and current coin of the United States, piracies, and felonies committed on the high seas, and offences against the law of nations, and no other crimes whatsoever; and it being true as a general principle, and one of the amendments to the Constitution having also declared, that "the powers not delegated to the United States by the Constitution, nor prohibited by it to the States, are reserved to the States respectively, or to the people," therefore . . . that the power to create, define, and punish such other crimes is reserved, and, of right, appertains solely and exclusively to the respective States, each within its own territory.

Resolved, . . . that no power over the freedom of religion, freedom of speech, or freedom of the press being delegated to the United States by the Constitution, nor prohibited by it to the States, all lawful powers respecting the same did of right remain, and were reserved to the

States or the people: that thus was manifested their determination to retain to themselves the right of judging how far the licentiousness of speech and of the press may be abridged without lessening their useful freedom, and how far those abuses which cannot be separated from their use should be tolerated, rather than the use destroyed. . . .

Resolved, That the construction applied by the General Government . . . to those parts of the Constitution of the United States which delegate to Congress a power "to lay and collect taxes, duties, imposts, and excises, to pay the debts, and provide for the common defence and general welfare of the United States," and "to make all laws which shall be necessary and proper for carrying into execution the powers vested by the Constitution in the government of the United States, or in any department or officer thereof," goes to the destruction of all limits prescribed to their power by the Constitution: that words meant by the instrument to be subsidiary only to the execution of limited powers, ought not to be so construed as themselves to give unlimited powers, nor a part to be so taken as to destroy the whole residue of that instrument. . . .

JEFFERSONIAN PRINCIPLES

Resolved, That . . . where powers are assumed which have not been delegated, a nullification is the rightful remedy. . . . — *Draft of the Kentucky Resolutions.* Vol. VII, pp. 289–301.

On State Governments

The true barriers of our liberty in this country are our State governments; and the wisest power ever contrived by man, is that of which our Revolution and present government found us possessed. Seventeen distinct States, amalgamated into one as to their foreign concerns, but single and independent as to their internal administration, regularly organized with legislature and governor resting on the choice of the people, and enlightened by a free press, can never be so fascinated by the arts of one man, as to submit voluntarily to his usurpation. Nor can they be constrained to it by any force he can possess. While that may paralyze the single State in which it happens to be encamped, sixteen others, spread over a country of two thousand miles diameter, rise up on every side, ready organized for deliberation by a constitutional legislature, and for action by their governor, constitutionally the commander of the militia of the State, that is to say, of every man in it able to bear arms. . . .

Dangers of another kind might more reasonably be apprehended from this perfect and distinct organization, civil and military, of the States; to wit, that certain States from local and occasional discontents, might attempt to secede from the Union. This is certainly possible; and would be befriended by this regular organization. But it is not probable that local discontents can spread to such an extent, as to be able to face the sound parts of so extensive an Union. — *Letter to A. C. V. Destutt De Tracy*, January 26, 1811. Vol. IX, pp. 308–309.

On the Central and State Governments

Our country is too large to have all its affairs directed by a single government. Public servants at such a distance, & from under the eye of their constituents, must, from the circumstances of distance, be unable to administer & overlook all the details necessary for the good government of the citizens, and the same circumstance, by rendering detection impossible to their constituents, will invite the public agents to corruption, plunder & waste. And I do verily believe, that if the principle were to prevail, of a common law being in force in the U. S. (which principle possesses the general government at once of all the powers of the state governments, and reduces us to a single consolidated government,) it would become the most corrupt government on the earth. You have seen the practises by which the public servants have been able to cover their conduct, or, where that could not be done, delusions by which they have varnished it for the eye of their constituents. What an augmentation of the field for jobbing, speculating, plundering, office-building & office-hunting would be produced by an assumption of all the state powers into the hands of the general government. The true theory of our constitution is surely the wisest & best, that the states are independent as to everything within themselves, & united as to everything respecting foreign nations. Let the general government be reduced to foreign concerns only, and let our affairs be disentangled from those of all other nations, except as to commerce, which the merchants will manage the better, the more they are left free to manage for themselves, and our general government may be reduced to a very simple organization, &

a very unexpensive one. — *Letter to Gideon Granger*, August 13, 1800. Vol. VII, pp. 451–452.

ON COÖPERATION WITH THE STATE GOVERNORS

Your opinion of the propriety & advantage of a more intimate correspondence between the executives of the several States, & that of the Union, as a central point, is precisely that which I have ever entertained; and on coming into office I felt the advantages which would result from that harmony. I had it even in contemplation, after the annual recommendation to Congress of those measures called for by the times, which the Constitution had placed under their power to make communications in like manner to the executives of the States, as to any parts of them to which the legislatures might be alone competent. For many are the exercises of power reserved to the States, wherein an uniformity of proceeding would be advantageous to all. Such are quarantines, health laws, regulations of the press, banking institutions, training militia, &c., &c. But you know what was the state of the several governments when I came into office. That a great proportion of them were federal, & would have been delighted with such opportunities of proclaiming their contempt, & of opposing republican men & measures. Opportunities so furnished & used by some of the State Governments, would have produced an ill effect, & would have insured the failure of the object of uniform proceeding. — *Letter to James Sullivan,* June 19, 1807.   Vol. IX, p. 76.

On the Judiciary

There was another amendment of which none of us thought at the time [1] and in the omission of which lurks the germ that is to destroy this happy combination of National powers in the General government for matters of National concern, and independent powers in the states for what concerns the states severally. In England it was a great point gained at the Revolution, that the commissions of the judges, which had hitherto been during pleasure, should thenceforth be made during good behavior. A Judiciary dependent on the will of the King had proved itself the most oppressive of all tools in the hands of that Magistrate. Nothing then could be more salutary than a change there

[1] The adoption of the Federal Constitution.

to the tenure of good behavior; and the question of good behavior left to the vote of a simple majority in the two houses of parliament. Before the revolution we were all good English Whigs, cordial in their free principles, and in their jealousies of their executive Magistrate. These jealousies are very apparent in all our state constitutions; and, in the general government in this instance, we have gone even beyond the English caution, by requiring a vote of two thirds in one of the Houses for removing a judge; a vote so impossible where any defence is made, before men of ordinary prejudices & passions, that our judges are effectually independent of the nation.[1] But this ought not to be. I would not indeed make them dependent on the Executive authority, as they formerly were in England; but I deem it indispensable to the continuance of this government that they should be submitted to some practical & impartial controul: and that this, to be impartial, must be compounded of a mixture of state and federal authorities. It is not enough that honest men are appointed judges. All know

[1] In the impeachment of judge Pickering of New Hampshire, a habitual & maniac drunkard, no defence was made. Had there been, the party vote more than one third of the Senate would have acquitted him. T. J.

the influence of interest on the mind of man, and how unconsciously his judgment is warped by that influence. To this bias add that of the esprit de corps, of their peculiar maxim and creed that "it is the office of a good judge to enlarge his jurisdiction," and the absence of responsibility, and how can we expect impartial decision between the General government, of which they are themselves so eminent a part, and an individual state from which they have nothing to hope or fear. We have seen too that, contrary to all correct example, they are in the habit of going out of the question before them, to throw an anchor ahead and grapple further hold for further advances of power. They are then in fact the corps of sappers & miners, steadily working to undermine the independent rights of the States, & to consolidate all power in the hands of that government in which they have so important a freehold estate. . . . I repeat that I do not charge the judges with wilful and ill-intentioned error; but honest error must be arrested where it's toleration leads to public ruin. As, for the safety of society, we commit honest maniacs to Bedlam, so judges should be withdrawn from their bench, whose erroneous biases are leading us to dissolution. — *Autobiography*. Vol. I, pp. 111–114.

The dignity and stability of government in all its branches, the morals of the people, and every blessing of society, depend so much upon an upright and skilful administration of justice, that the judicial power ought to be distinct from both the legislature and executive, and independent upon both, that so it may be a check upon both, as both should be checks upon that. The judges, therefore, should always be men of learning and experience in the laws, of exemplary morals, great patience, calmness and attention; their minds should not be distracted with jarring interests; they should not be dependent upon any man or body of men. To these ends they should hold estates for life in their offices, or, in other words, their commissions should be during good behavior, and their salaries ascertained and established by law. — *Letter to George Wythe*, July [?] 1776. Vol. II, p. 59.

On the Treaty-making Power

He [Minister Genet] asked if they [Congress] were not the sovereign. I told him so, [*sic*] they were sovereign in making laws only, the executive was sovereign in executing them, and the judiciary in construing them where they related to their department. "But," said he, "at least, Congress are bound to see that the treaties are observed." I told him no; there were very few cases indeed arising out of treaties, which they could take notice of; that the President is to see that treaties are observed. "If he decides against the treaty, to whom is a nation to appeal?" I told him the constitution had made the President the last appeal. — *The Anas*. Vol. I, p. 239.

I insisted that in giving to the President & Senate a power to make treaties, the constitution meant only to authorize them to carry into effect by way of treaty any powers they might constitutionally exercise. I was sensible of the weak points in this position, but there were still weaker in the other hypotheses, and if it be impossible to discover a rational measure of authority to have been given by this clause, I would rather suppose that the cases which my hypothesis would leave unprovided, were not thought of by the Convention, or if thought of, could not be agreed on, or were thought on

and deemed unnecessary to be invested in the
government. Of this last description were
treaties of neutrality, treaties of offensive &
defensive &c. In every event I would rather
construe so narrowly as to oblige the nation to
amend and thus declare what powers they
would agree to yield, than too broadly & indeed
so broadly as to enable the Executive and Senate
to do things which the constitution forbids. —
The Anas. Vol. I, p. 269.

On the Constitution and Presidential Term

I am not a Federalist, because I never submitted the whole system of my opinions to the
creed of any party of men whatever in religion,
in philosophy, in politics, or in anything else
where I was capable of thinking for myself.
Such an addiction is the last degradation of a
free and moral agent. If I could not go to
heaven but with a party, I would not go there
at all. Therefore I protest to you I am not
of the party of the federalists. But I am much
farther from that of the Antifederalists. I
approved, from the first moment, of the great
mass of what is in the new constitution, the

consolidation of the government, the organization into Executive legislative & judiciary, the subdivision of the legislative, the happy compromise between the great & little states by the different manner of voting in the different houses, the voting by persons instead of states, the qualified negative on laws given to the Executive, which however I should have liked better if associated with the judiciary also as in New York, and the power of taxation. I thought at first that the latter might have been limited. A little reflection soon convinced me it ought not to be. What I disapproved from the first moment also was the want of a bill of rights to guard liberty against the legislative as well as executive branches of the government, that is to say to secure freedom in religion, freedom of the press, freedom from monopolies, freedom from unlawful imprisonment, freedom from a permanent military, and a trial by jury in all cases determinable by the laws of the land. I disapproved also the perpetual reeligibility of the President. To these points of disapprobation I adhere. . . . With respect to re-eligibility of the president, I find myself differing from the majority of my countrymen, for I think there are but three states out of the 11. which have desired an alteration of this. And indeed, since the thing is established, I would wish it not to be altered during the life of our great leader, whose executive talents are superior to those I believe of any man in the world, and who alone by the authority of his name and the confidence reposed in his perfect integrity, is fully qualified to put the new government so under way as to secure it against the efforts of opposition. But having derived from our error all the good there was in it I hope we shall correct it the moment we can no longer have the same name at the helm. — *Letter to Francis Hopkinson,* March 13, 1789. Vol. V, pp. 76–78.

On the Presidential Term

The second feature I dislike, and greatly dislike, is the abandonment in every instance of the necessity of rotation in office, and most particularly in the case of the President. Experience concurs with reason in concluding that the first magistrate will always be re-elected if the Constitution permits it. He is then an officer for life. This once observed, it becomes of so much consequence to certain nations to have a friend or a foe at the head

of our affairs that they will interfere with money
& with arms.   A Galloman or an Angloman will
be supported by the nation he befriends.   If
once elected, and at a second or third election
out voted by one or two votes, he will pretend
false votes, foul play, hold possession of the
reins of government, be supported by the
States voting for him, especially if they are the
central ones lying in a compact body themselves
& separating their opponents: and they will
be aided by one nation of Europe, while the
majority are aided by another.   The election
of a President of America some years hence will
be much more interesting to certain nations
of Europe than ever the election of a king of
Poland was.   Reflect on all the instances in
history antient & modern, of elective monarchies,
and say if they do not give foundation for my
fears.   The Roman emperors, the popes, while
they were of any importance, the German
emperors till they became hereditary in practice, the kings of Poland, the Deys of the
Ottoman dependencies.   It may be said that
if elections are to be attended with these
disorders, the seldomer they are renewed the
better.   But experience shews that the only
way to prevent disorder is to render them

uninteresting by frequent changes. An incapacity to be elected a second time would
have been the only effectual preventive. The
power of removing him every fourth year by
the vote of the people is a power which will not
be exercised. The king of Poland is removeable
every day by the Diet, yet he is never removed.
— *Letter to James Madison*, December 20, 1787.
Vol. IV, pp. 477–478.

My wish therefore was that the President
should be elected for 7 years & be ineligible
afterwards. This term I thought sufficient to
enable him, with the concurrence of the legislature, to carry thro' & establish any system of
improvement he should propose for the general
good. But the practice adopted I think is
better allowing his continuance for 8 years with
a liability to be dropped at half way of the term,
making that a period of probation. That his
continuance should be restrained to 7 years was
the opinion of the Convention at an early stage
of it's sessions, when it voted that term by a
majority of 8 against 2 and by a simple majority
that he should be ineligible a second time.
This opinion was confirmed by the house so late
as July 26, referred to the committee of detail,

reported favorably by them, and changed to the present form by final vote on the last day but one only of their session.[1] Of this change three states expressed their disapprobation, N. York by recommending an amendment that the President should not be eligible a third time, and Virginia and N. Carolina that he should not be capable of serving more than 8 in any term of 16 years. And altho' this amendment has not been made in form, yet practice seems to have established it. The example of 4 Presidents voluntarily retiring at the end of their 8th year, & the progress of public opinion that the principle is salutary, have given it in practice the force of precedent & usage; insomuch that should a President consent to be a candidate for a 3d election, I trust he would be rejected on this demonstration of ambitious views. — *Autobiography*. Vol. I, pp. 110–111.

My opinion originally was that the President of the U. S., should have been elected for 7 years, & forever ineligible afterwards. I have since become sensible that 7 years is too long to be irremovable, and that there should be a peaceable way of withdrawing a man in midway

[1] There is a slight error here in date.

who is doing wrong. The service for 8 years
with a power to remove at the end of the first
four, comes nearly to my principle as corrected
by experience. And it is in adherence to that
that I am determined to withdraw at the end of
my second term. The danger is that the
indulgence & attachments of the people will
keep a man in the chair after he becomes a
dotard, that reelection through life shall become habitual, & election for life follow that.
Genl. Washington set the example of volun-
tary retirement after 8 years. I shall follow
it, and a few more precedents will oppose the
obstacle of habit to anyone after a while who
shall endeavor to extend his term. Perhaps
it may beget a disposition to establish it by an
amendment of the constitution. I believe I
am doing right, therefore, in pursuing my principle. I had determined to declare my intention, but I have consented to be silent on the
opinion of friends, who think it best not to
put a continuance out of my power in defiance
of all circumstances. There is, however, but
one circumstance which could engage my
acquiescence in another election, to wit, such
a division about a successor as might bring
in a Monarchist. But this circumstance is

JEFFERSONIAN PRINCIPLES

impossible. While, therefore, I shall make no formal declarations to the public of my purpose, I have freely let it be understood in private conversation. — *Letter to John Taylor,* January 6, 1805. Vol. VIII, p. 339.

That I should lay down my charge at a proper period, is as much a duty as to have borne it faithfully. If some termination to the services of the chief magistrate be not fixed by the Constitution, or supplied by practice, his office, nominally for years, will, in fact, become for life; and history shows how easily that degenerates into an inheritance. Believing that a representative government, responsible at short periods of election, is that which produces the greatest sum of happiness to mankind, I feel it a duty to do no act which shall essentially impair that principle; and I should unwillingly be the person who, disregarding the sound precedent set by an illustrious predecessor, should furnish the first example of prolongation beyond the second term of office. — *Jefferson's declination to serve a third term.* Quoted by John Sharp Williams in *Thomas Jefferson* (1913), p. 169.

JEFFERSONIAN PRINCIPLES

On the President's Cabinet

Our government although in theory subject to be directed by the unadvised will of the President, is, and from its origin has been, a very different thing in practice. The minor business in each department is done by the head of the department on consultation with the President alone; but all matters of importance or difficulty are submitted to all the heads of departments composing the cabinet. Sometimes, by the President's consulting them separately and successively, as they happen to call on him, but in the gravest cases calling them together, discussing the subject maturely, and finally taking the vote, on which the President counts himself but as one. So that in all important cases the Executive is in fact a directory, which certainly the President might control; but of this there was never an example either in the first or the present administration. — *Letter to William Short*, June 12, 1807. Vol. IX, pp. 69–70.

JEFFERSONIAN PRINCIPLES

On the Common Law and the Seat of Sovereignty

Of all the doctrines which have ever been broached by the federal government, the novel one, of the common law being in force & cognizable as an existing law in their courts, is to me the most formidable. All their other assumptions of un-given powers have been in the detail. The bank law, the treaty doctrine, the sedition act, the alien act, the undertaking to change the state laws of evidence in the state courts by certain parts of the stamp act, &c., &c., have been solitary, unconsequential, timid things in comparison with the audacious, barefaced and sweeping pretension to a system of law for the U. S., without the adoption of their legislature, and so infinitively [*sic*] beyond their power to adopt. If this assumption be yielded to, the state courts may shut up, as there will then be nothing to hinder citizens of the same state suing each other in the federal courts in every case, as on a bond for instance, because the common law obliges payment of it, & the common law they say is their law. I am happy you have taken up the subject; & I have carefully perused & considered the notes you enclosed, and find but a single paragraph which I do not approve. It is that wherein (page 2) you say, that laws being emanations from the legislative department, &, when once enacted, continuing in force from a presumption that their will so continues, that that presumption fails & the laws of course fall, on the destruction of that legislative department. I do not think this is the true bottom on which laws & the administering them rest. The whole body of the nation is the sovereign legislative, judiciary and executive power for itself. The inconvenience of meeting to exercise these powers in person, and their inaptitude to exercise them, induce them to appoint special organs to declare their legislative will, to judge & to execute it. It is the will of the nation which makes the law obligatory; it is their will which creates or annihilates the organ which is to declare & announce it. They may do it by a single person, as an Emperor of Russia, (constituting his declarations evidence of their will,) or by a few persons, as the Aristocracy of Venice, or by a complication of councils, as in our former regal government, or our present republican one. The law being law because it is the will of the nation, is not changed by their changing the organ through which they chuse to announce their future will; no more than the acts I have done by one attorney lose their obligation by my changing or discontinuing that attorney. This doctrine has been, in a certain degree sanctioned by the federal executive. For it is precisely that on which the continuance of obligation from our treaty with France was established, and the doctrine was particularly developed in a letter to Gouverneur Morris, written with the approbation of President Washington and his cabinet. Mercer once prevailed on the Virginia Assembly to declare a different doctrine in some resolutions. These met universal disapprobation in this, as well as the other States, and if I mistake not, a subsequent Assembly did something to do away the authority of their former unguarded resolutions. In this case, as in all others, the true principle will be quite as effectual to establish the just deductions, for before the revolution, the nation of Virginia had, by the organs they then thought proper to constitute, established a system of laws, which they divided into three denominations of 1, common law; 2, statute law; 3, Chancery: or if you please, into two only, of 1, common law; 2, Chancery. When,

by the declaration of Independence, they chose
to abolish their former organs of declaring their
will, the acts of will already formally & constitutionally declared, remained untouched.
For the nation was not dissolved, was not anni-
hilated; it's will, therefore, remained in full
vigor; and on the establishing the new organs,
first of a convention, & afterwards a more
complicated legislature, the old acts of national
will continued in force, until the nation should,
by its new organs, declare it's will changed.
The common law, therefore, which was not in
force when we landed here, nor till we had
formed ourselves into a nation, and had manifested by the organs we constituted that the
common law was to be our law, continued to be
our law, because the nation continued in being,
& because though it changed the organs for the
future declarations of its will, yet it did not
change its former declarations that the common
law was it's law. Apply these principles to
the present case. Before the revolution there
existed no such nation as the U. S.; they then
first associated as a nation, but for special
purposes only. They had all their laws to make,
as Virginia had on her first establishment as a
nation. But they did not, as Virginia had done,

proceed to adopt a whole system of laws ready
made to their hand. As their association as a
nation was only for special purposes, to wit,
for the management of their concerns with one
another & with foreign nations, and the states
composing the association chose to give it
powers for those purposes & no others, they
could not adopt any general system, because it
would have embraced objects on which this association had no right to form or declare a will.
It was not the organ for declaring a national will
in these cases. In the cases confided to them,
they were free to dec'are the will of the nation,
the law; but till it was declared there could be no
law. So that the common law did not become,
ipso facto, law on the new association; it could
only become so by a positive adoption, & so far
only as they were authorized to adopt.

I think it will be of great importance, when
you come to the proper part, to portray at
full length the consequences of this new doctrine,
that the common law is the law of the U. S., &
that their courts have, of course, jurisdiction
co-extensive with that law, that is to say,
general over all cases & persons. But, great
heavens! Who could have conceived in 1789
that within ten years we should have to combat

such windmills. — *Letter to Edmund Randolph,* August 18, 1799. Vol. VII, pp. 383–387.

ON THE ALIENATION OF TERRITORY

I considered . . . that the Executive with either or both branches of the legislature could not alien any part of our territory: that by the Law of nations it was settled that the Unity & indivisibility of the society was so fundamental that it could not be dismembered by the Constituted authorities, except 1. where *all power* was delegated to them (as in the case of despotic governments) or 2. where it was expressly delegated. That neither of these delegations had been made to our general government & therefore that it had no right to dismember or alienate any portion of territory once ultimately consolidated with us: and that we could no more cede to the Indians than to the English or Spaniards, as it might according to acknowledged principles remain as irrevocably and eternally with the one as the other. — *The Anas.* Vol. I, p. 219.

ON PUBLIC OFFICERS AND THE LAW

The question you propose, whether circumstances do not sometimes occur, which make it a duty in officers of high trust, to assume authorities beyond the law, is easy of solution in principle, but sometimes embarrassing in practice. A strict observance of the written laws is doubtless *one* of the high duties of a good citizen, but it is not *the highest*. The laws of necessity, of self-preservation, of saving our country when in danger, are of higher obligation. To lose our country by a scrupulous adherence to written law, would be to lose the law itself, with life, liberty, property and all those who are enjoying them with us; thus absurdly sacrificing the end to the means. . . .

From these examples and principles you may see what I think on the question proposed. They do not go to the case of persons charged with petty duties, where consequences are trifling, and time allowed for a legal course, nor to authorize them to take such cases out of the written law. In these, the example of over-leaping the law is of greater evil than a strict adherence to its imperfect provisions. It is incumbent on those only who accept of great charges, to risk themselves on great occasions, when the safety of the nation, or some of its very high interests are at stake. . . . The line of discrimination between cases may be difficult; but the good officer is bound to draw it at his own peril, and throw himself on the justice of his country and the rectitude of his motives. — *Letter to John B. Colvin*, September 20, 1810.   Vol. IX, pp. 279–280.

On the Louisiana Purchase

This treaty [purchasing the Louisiana territory from France] must of course be laid before both Houses, because both have important functions to exercise respecting it. They, I presume, will see their duty to their country in ratifying & paying for it, so as to secure a good which would otherwise probably be never again in their power. But I suppose they must then appeal to *the nation* for an additional article to the Constitution, approving & confirming an act which the nation had not previously authorized.   The constitution has made no provision for our holding foreign territory, still less for incorporating foreign nations into our Union. The Executive in seizing the fugitive occurrence which so much advances the good of their country, have done an act beyond the Constitution.   The Legislature in casting behind them metaphysical subtleties, and risking themselves like faithful servants,

must ratify & pay for it, and throw themselves
on their country for doing for them unauthorized
what we know they would have done for themselves had they been in a situation to do it.   It
is the case of a guardian, investing the money
of his ward in purchasing an important adjacent
territory; & saying to him when of age, I did
this for your good; I pretend to no right to
bind you: you may disavow me, and I must
get out of the scrape as I can: I thought it my
duty to risk myself for you.   But we shall not
be disavowed by the nation, and their act of
indemnity will confirm & not weaken the
Constitution, by more strongly marking out its
lines. — *Letter to John C. Breckenridge*, August
12, 1803.   Vol. VIII, p. 244.

On the Public Purse

The purse of the people is the real seat of
sensibility.   It is to be drawn upon largely, and
they will then listen to truths which could not
excite them through any other organ. — *Letter
to Archibald H. Rowan*, September 26, 1798.
Vol. VII, p. 281.

JEFFERSONIAN PRINCIPLES

ON THE POWER OF BORROWING

I wish it were possible to obtain a single amendment to our constitution. I would be willing to depend on that alone for the reduction of the administration of our government to the genuine principles of it's constitution; I mean an additional article, taking from the federal government the power of borrowing. I now deny their power of making paper money or anything else a legal tender. I know that to pay all proper expences within the year, would, in case of war, be hard on us. But not so hard as ten wars instead of one. For wars would be reduced in that proportion; besides that the State governments would be free to lend *their credit* in borrowing quotas. . . . It is a singular phenomenon, that while our State governments are the very *best in the world*, without exception or comparison, our general government has, in the rapid course of 9. or 10. years, become more arbitrary, has swallowed more of the public liberty than even that of England. — *Letter to John Taylor*, November 26, 1798. Vol. VII, pp. 310–311. [Written at the time of the Alien and Sedition Laws. — Ed.]

JEFFERSONIAN PRINCIPLES

On Debt and the Binding of Future Generations

The question Whether one generation of men has a right to bind another, seems never to have been started either on this or our side of the water.[1] Yet it is a question of such consequences as not only to merit decision, but place also, among the fundamental principles of every government. . . . I set out on this ground which I suppose to be self-evident, *"that the earth belongs in usufruct to the living;"* that the dead have neither powers nor rights over it. The portion occupied by any individual ceases to be his when himself ceases to be, and reverts to society. . . . No man can by *natural right* oblige the lands he occupied, or the persons who succeed him in that occupation, to the paiment of debts contracted by him. For if he could, he might during his own life, eat up the usufruct of the lands for several generations to come, and then the lands would belong to the dead, and not to the living, which would be reverse of our principle. What is true of every member of the society individually, is true of them all collectively, since the rights

[1] Jefferson was writing from Paris.

of the whole can be no more than the sum of the rights of the individuals. . . . Suppose Louis XV. and his contemporary generation had said to the money lenders of Genoa, give us money that we may eat, drink, and be merry in our day; and on condition you will demand no interest till the end of 19. years, you shall then forever after receive an annual interest of 12.5 per cent. The money is lent on these conditions, is divided among the living, eaten, drank, and squandered. Would the present generation be obliged to apply the produce of the earth and of their labour to replace their dissipations? Not at all. I suppose that the received opinion, that the public debts of one generation devolve on the next, has been suggested by our seeing habitually in private life that he who succeeds to lands is required to pay the debts of his ancestor or testator, without considering that this requisition is municipal only, not moral, flowing from the will of the society which has found it convenient to appropriate the lands become vacant by the death of their occupant on the condition of a paiment of his debts; but that between society and society, or generation and generation there is no municipal obligation, no umpire but the law of nature.

JEFFERSONIAN PRINCIPLES

We seem not to have perceived that, by the law of nature, one generation is to another as one independent nation to another. . . . On similar ground it may be proved that no society can make a perpetual constitution, or even a perpetual law. The earth belongs always to the living generation. They manage it then, and what proceeds from it, as they please, during their usufruct. They are masters too of their own persons, and consequently may govern them as they please. But persons and property make the sum of the objects of government. The constitution and the laws of their predecessors extinguished them, in their natural course, with those whose will gave them being. This could preserve that being till it ceased to be itself, and no longer. Every constitution, then, and every law, naturally expires at the end of 19. years. If it be enforced longer, it is an act of force and not of right. . . .

Turn this subject in your mind, my Dear Sir, and particularly as to the power of contracting debts. . . . At first blush it may be rallied as a theoretical speculation; but examination will prove it to be solid and salutary. It would furnish matter for a fine preamble to our first law for appropriating the public revenue; and it will exclude, at the threshold of our new government the contagious and ruinous errors of this quarter of the globe, which have armed despots with means not sanctioned by nature for binding in chains their fellow-men. We have already given, in example one effectual check to the Dog of war, by transferring the power of letting him loose from the executive to the Legislative body, from those who are to spend to those who are to pay. I should be pleased to see this second obstacle held out by us also in the first instance. No nation can make a declaration against the validity of long-contracted debts so disinterestedly as we, since we do not owe a shilling which may not be paid with ease principal and interest, within the time of our own lives. — *Letter to James Madison*, September 6, 1789. Vol. V, pp. 115–123.

That we are bound to defray its expenses [the Revolutionary War] within our own time, and unauthorized to burden posterity with them, I suppose to have been proved in my former letter. I will place the question nevertheless in one additional point of view. The former regarded their independent right over the earth; this over their own persons. There have existed nations, and civilized and learned nations, who have thought a father had a right to sell his child as a slave, in perpetuity; that he could alienate his body and industry conjointly, and *a fortiori* his industry separately; and consume its fruits himself. A nation asserting this fratricide right might well suppose they could burthen with public as well as private debt their *"nati na orum, et qui nascentur ab illis."* But we, this age, and in this country especially are advanced beyond those notions of natural law. We acknowledge that our children are born free; that that freedom is the gift of nature, and not of him who begot them; that though under our care during infancy, and therefore of necessity under a duly tempered authority, that care is confided to us to be exercised for the preservation and good of the child only; and his labors during youth are given as a retribution for the charges of infancy. As he never was the property of his father, so when adult he is *sui juris*, entitled himself to the use of his own limbs and the fruits of his own exertions: so far we are advanced, without mind enough, it seems to take the whole step. We believe, or we act as if we believed, that although an individual father cannot alienate the labor of his son, the aggregate body of fathers may alienate the labor of all their sons, of their posterity, in the aggregate, and oblige them to pay for all the enterprises, just or unjust, profitable or ruinous, into which our vices, our passions, or our personal interests may lead us. But I trust that this proposition needs only to be looked at by an American to be seen in its true point of view, and that we shall consider ourselves unauthorized to saddle posterity with our debts, and morally bound to pay them ourselves; and consequently within what may be deemed the period of a generation, or the life of the majority. In my former letter I supposed this to be a little over twenty years. We must raise then ourselves the money for this war, either by taxes within the year, or by loans; and if by loans, we must repay them ourselves, proscribing forever the English practice of perpetual funding; the ruinous consequences of which, putting right out of the question, should be a sufficient warning to a considerate nation to avoid the example. — *Letter to John Wilson*, August 17, 1813. Vol. IX, pp. 396–397.

JEFFERSONIAN PRINCIPLES

On Suspension of Habeas Corpus

Why suspend the Habeas Corpus in insurrections & rebellions? The parties who may be arrested may be charged instantly with a well defined crime, of course the judge will remand them. If publick safety requires that the government should have a man imprisoned on less probable testimony in those than in other emergencies; let him be taken & tried, retaken & retried, while the necessity continues, only giving him redress against the government for damages. Examine the history of England. See how few cases of the suspension of the Habeas corpus law have been worthy of that suspension. They have been either real treasons wherein the parties might as well have been charged at once, or sham plots where it was shameful they should ever have been suspected. Yet for the few cases wherein the suspension of the habeas corpus has done real good, that operation is now become habitual, & the minds of the nation prepared to live under its constant suspension. — *Letter to James Madison*, July 31, 1788. Vol. V, pp. 46–47.

JEFFERSONIAN PRINCIPLES

On Commerce and Manufactures

You ask what I think on the expediency of encouraging our states to be commercial? Were I to indulge my own theory, I should wish them to practise neither commerce nor navigation, but to stand with respect to Europe precisely on the footing of China. We should thus avoid wars, and all our citizens would be husbandmen. Whenever indeed our numbers should so increase as that our produce would overstock the markets of those nations who should come to seek it, the farmers must either employ the surplus of their time in manufactures, or the surplus of our hands must be employed in manufactures, or in navigation. But that day would, I think be distant, and we should long keep our workmen in Europe, while Europe should be drawing rough materials & even subsistence from America. But this is theory only, & a theory which the servants of America are not at liberty to follow. Our people have a decided taste for navigation & commerce. They take this from their mother country: & their servants are in duty bound to calculate all their measures on this datum: we wish to do it by throwing open all the doors of commerce & knocking off its shackles. But as this cannot be done for others, unless they will do it for us, & there is no great probability that Europe will do this, I suppose we shall be obliged to adopt a system which may shackle them in their ports as they do us in ours. — *Letter to Count van Hogendorp*, October 13, 1785. Vol. IV, p. 105.

On Commerce and Tariffs

Such being the restrictions on the commerce and navigation of the United States; the question is, in what way they may best be removed, modified, or counteracted?

As to commerce, two methods occur. 1. By friendly arrangements with the several nations with whom these restrictions exist; Or, 2. By the separate act of own legislatures for countervailing their effects.

There can be no doubt but that of these two, friendly arrangements is the most eligible. Instead of embarrassing commerce under piles of regulating laws, duties and prohibitions, could it be relieved from all its shackles in all parts of the world, could every country be employed in producing that which nature has best fitted it to produce, and each be free to exchange with others mutual surplusses for mutual wants, the greatest possible would then be produced of those things which contribute to human life and human happiness; the numbers of mankind would be increased, and their condition bettered. Would even a single nation begin with the United States this system of free commerce, it would be advisable to begin it with that nation; since it is only one by one that it can be extended to all. . . . But should any nation, contrary to our wishes, suppose it may better find its advantage by continuing its system of prohibitions, duties and regulations, it behooves us to protect our citizens, their commerce and navigation, by counter prohibitions, duties and regulations also. Free commerce and navigation are not to be given in exchange for restrictions and vexations; nor are they likely to produce a relaxation of them.

Our navigation involves still higher considerations. As a branch of industry, it is valuable, but as a resource of defence, essential. . . . Were the ocean, which is the common property of all, open to the industry of all, so that every person and vessel should be free to take employment wherever it could be found, the United

States would certainly not set the example of appropriating to themselves, exclusively, any portion of the common stock of occupation. They would rely on the enterprise and activity of their citizens for a due participation of the benefits of the seafaring business, and for keeping the marine class of citizens equal to their object.   But if particular nations grasp at undue shares, and, more especially, if they seize on the means of the United States, to convert them into aliment for their own strength, and withdraw them entirely from the support of those to whom they belong, defensive and protecting measures become necessary on the part of the nation whose marine resources are thus invaded. . . .

It is true we must expect some inconvenience in practice from the establishment of discriminating duties.   But in this, as in so many other cases, we are left to choose between two evils. These inconveniences are nothing when weighed against the loss of wealth and loss of force, which will follow our perseverance in the plan of indiscrimination.   When once it shall be perceived that we are either in the system or habit of giving equal advantages to those who extinguish our commerce and navigation by duties and prohibitions, as to those who treat both with liberality and justice, liberality and justice will be converted by all into duties and prohibitions. It is not to the moderation and justice of others we are to trust for fair and equal access to market with our productions, or for our due share in the transportation of them; but to our own means of independence, and the firm will to create them. Nor do the inconveniences of discrimination merit consideration. Not one of the nations before mentioned, perhaps not a commercial nation on earth, is without them. In our case one distinction alone will suffice: that is to say, between nations who favor our productions and navigation and those who do not favor them. One set of moderate duties, say the present duties, for the first, and a fixed advance on these as to some articles, and prohibitions as to others, for the last. — *Report on the Privileges and Restrictions on the Commerce of the United States in Foreign Countries.* December 16, 1793. Vol. VI, pp. 480–483.

On Manufactures

You tell me I am quoted by those who wish to continue our dependence on England for manufactures. There was a time when I might have been so quoted with more candor, but within the thirty years which have since elapsed, how are circumstances changed! We were then in peace. Our independent place among nations was acknowledged. A commerce which offered the raw material in exchange for the same material after receiving the last touch of industry, was worthy of welcome to all nations. It was expected that those especially to whom manufacturing industry was important, would cherish the friendship of such customers by every favor, by every inducement, and particularly cultivate their peace by every act of justice and friendship. Under this prospect, the question seemed legitimate, whether, with such an immensity of unimproved land, courting the hand of husbandry, the industry of agriculture, or that of manufactures, would add most to the national wealth? And the doubt was entertained on this consideration chiefly, that to the labor of the husbandman a vast addition is made by the spontaneous energies of the earth on which it is employed: for one grain of wheat committed to the earth, she renders twenty, thirty, and even fifty fold, whereas to the labor of the manufacturer nothing is added. Pounds of flax, in his hands, yield, on the contrary but pennyweights of lace. This exchange, too, laborious as it might seem, what a field did it promise for the occupations of the ocean; what a nursery for that class of citizens who were to exercise and maintain our equal rights on that element? This was the state of things in 1785, when the "Notes on Virginia" were first printed; when, the ocean being open to all nations, and their common right in it acknowledged by the assent and usage of all, it was thought that the doubt might claim some consideration. But who in 1785 could foresee the rapid depravity which was to render the close of that century the disgrace of the history of man? Who could have imagined that the two most distinguished in the rank of nations, for science and civilization, would have suddenly descended from that honorable eminence, and setting at defiance all those moral laws established by the Author of nature between nation and nation, as between man and man, would cover earth and sea with robberies and piracies, merely because strong enough to do it with temporal impunity; and that under this disbandment of nations from social order, we should have been despoiled of a thousand ships, and have thousands of our citizens reduced to Algerine slavery. [The war between England and France and their depredations upon us.] Yet all this has taken place. . . . We were completely excluded from the ocean. Compare this state of things with that of '85, and say whether an opinion founded in the circumstances of that day can be fairly applied to those of the present. We have experienced what we did not then believe, that there exists both profligacy and power enough to exclude us from the field of interchange with other nations: that to be independent for the comforts of life we must fabricate them ourselves. We must now place the manufacturer by the side of the agriculturist. The former question is suppressed, or rather assumes a new form. Shall we make our own comforts, or go without them, at the will of a foreign nation? He, therefore, who is now against domestic manufacture, must be for reducing us either to dependence on that foreign nation, or to be clothed in skins, and to live like wild beasts in dens and caverns. I am not one of these; experience has taught me that manufactures are now as necessary to our independence as to our comfort; and if those who quote me as of a different opinion, will keep pace with me in purchasing nothing foreign where an equivalent of domestic fabric can be obtained, without regard to difference of price, it will not be our fault, if we do not soon have a supply at home equal to our demand, and wrest that weapon of distress from the hand which has wielded it. If it be proposed to go beyond our own supply, the question of '85 will then recur, will our *surplus* labor be then most beneficially employed in the culture of the earth, or in the fabrications of art? We have time yet for consideration, before that question will press upon us; and the maxim to be applied will depend on the circumstances which shall then exist; for in so complicated a science as political economy, no one axiom can be laid down as wise and expedient for all times and circumstances, and for their contraries. — *Letter to Benjamin Austin*, January 9, 1816. Vol. X, pp. 8–10.

On Laissez-Faire

Agriculture, manufactures, commerce, and navigation, the four pillars of our prosperity, are the most thriving when left free to individual enterprise. Protection from casual embarrassments, however, may sometimes be seasonably interposed. — *First annual message to Congress,* December 8, 1801.   Vol. VIII, p. 123.

On Banking

In the revolutionary war, the old Congress and the States issued bills without interest, and without tax.   They occupied the channels of circulation very freely, till those channels were overflowed by an excess beyond all the calls of circulation.   But although we have so improvidently suffered the field of circulating medium to be filched from us by private individuals, yet I think we may recover it in part, and even in the whole, if the States will co-operate with us. . . .

In this way, I am not without a hope, that this great, this sole resource for loans in an agricultural country, might yet be recovered for the use of the nation during war; and, if obtained *in perpetuum,* it would always be sufficient to carry us through any war; provided, that in the interval between war and war, all the outstanding paper should be called in, coin permitted to flow in again, and to hold the field of circulation until another war should require its yielding place again to the national medium.

But it will be asked, are we to have no banks? Are merchants and others to be deprived of the resource of short accomodations, found so convenient? I answer, let us have banks; but let them be such as are alone to be found in any country on earth, except Great Britain. There is not a bank of discount on the continent of Europe, (at least there was not one when I was there,) which offers anything but cash in exchange for discounted bills. . . . It is from Great Britain we copy the idea of giving paper in exchange for discounted bills. . . . The unlimited emission of bank paper has banished all her specie, and is now, by a depreciation acknowledged by her own statesmen, carrying her rapidly to bankruptcy, as it did France, as it did us, and will do us again, and every country permitting paper to be circulated, other than that by public authority, rigorously limited to the just measure for circulation. — *Letter to John Wayles Eppes*, June 24, 1813. Vol. IX, pp. 392–394.

On Naval Force

But how dreadfully we shall suffer on our coasts, if we have no force on the water, former experience has taught us. Indeed I look forward with horror to the very possible case of war with an European power, & think there is no protection against them but from the possession of some force on the sea. Our vicinity to their West India possessions & to the fisheries is a bridle which a small naval force on our part would hold in the mouths of the most powerful of these countries. I hope our land office will rid us of our debts, & that our first attention then will be to the beginning a naval force of some sort. This alone can countenance our people as carriers on the water, & I suppose them to be determined to continue such. — *Letter to John Jay*, August 23, 1785. Vol. IV, p. 90.

ON THE EMBARGO

The idea seems to gain credit that the naval powers combined against France will prohibit supplies even of provisions to that country. Should this be formally notified I should suppose Congress would be called, because it is a justifiable cause of war, & as the Executive cannot decide the question of war on the affirmative side, neither ought it to do so on the negative side, by preventing the competent body from deliberating on the question. But I should hope that war would not be their choice. I think it will furnish us a happy opportunity of setting another example to the world, by shewing that nations may be brought to do justice by appeals to their interests as well as by appeals to arms. I should hope that Congress instead of a denunciation of war, would instantly exclude from our ports all the manufactures, produce, vessels & subjects of the nations committing this aggression, during the continuance of the aggression & till full satisfaction made for it. This would work well in many ways, safely in all, & introduce between nations another umpire than war. It would relieve us too from the risks & the horrors of cutting throats. — *Letter to James Madison*, March, 1793. Vol. VI, p. 192.

On Slavery

I had always hoped that the younger generation receiving their early impressions after the flame of liberty had been kindled in every breast, & had become as it were the vital spirit of every American, that the generous temperament of youth, analogous to the motion of their blood, and above the suggestions of avarice, would have sympathized with oppression, and found their love of liberty beyond their own share in it. But my intercourse with them, since my return has not been sufficient to ascertain that they had made towards this point the progress I had hoped. Your solitary but welcome voice is the first which had brought this sound to my ear; and I have considered the general silence which prevails on this subject as indicating an apathy unfavorable to every hope. Yet the hour of emancipation is advancing, in the march of time. It will come; and whether brought on by the generous energy of our own minds; or by the bloody process of St. Domingo, excited and conducted by the power of our present enemy, if once stationed permanently within our country, and offering asylum & arms to the oppressed, is a leaf of our history not yet turned over. As to the method by which this difficult work is to be effected, if permitted to be done by ourselves, I have seen no proposition so expedient on the whole, as that of emancipation of those born after a given day, and of their education and expatriation after a given age. This would give time for a gradual extinction of that species of labor & substitution of another, and lessen the severity of the shock which an operation so fundamental cannot fail to produce. For men probably of any color, but of this color we know, brought from their infancy without necessity for thought or forecast, are by their habits rendered as incapable as children of taking care of themselves, and are extinguished promptly wherever industry is necessary for raising young. In the mean time they are pests in society by their idleness, and the depredations to which this leads them. Their amalgamation with the other color produces a degradation to which no lover of his country, no lover of excellence in the human character can innocently consent. . . . My opinion has ever been that, until more can be done for them, we should endeavor, with those whom fortune has thrown on our hands, to feed and clothe them well, protect them from all ill usage, require such reasonable labor only as is performed voluntarily by freemen, & be led by no repugnancies to abdicate them, and our duties to them. The laws do not permit us to turn them loose, if that were for their good: and to commute them for other property is to commit them to those whose usage of them we cannot control. — *Letter to Edward Coles*, August 25, 1814. Vol. IX, pp. 478–479.

JEFFERSONIAN PRINCIPLES

The bill on the subject of slaves was a mere digest of the existing laws respecting them, without any intimation of a plan for a future & general emancipation. It was thought better that this should be kept back, and attempted only by way of amendment whenever the bill should be brought on. The principles of the amendment however were agreed on, that is to say, the freedom of all born after a certain day, and deportation at a proper age. But it was found that the public mind would not bear the proposition, nor will it bear it even at this day. Yet the day is not far distant when it must bear and adopt it, or worse will follow. Nothing is more certainly written in the book of fate than that these people are to be free. Nor is it less certain that the two races, equally free, cannot live in the same government. Nature, habit, opinion has drawn indelible lines of distinction between them. It is still in our power to direct the process of emancipation and deportation peaceably and in such slow degree as that the evil will wear off insensibly, and their place be pari passu filled up by white laborers. If on the contrary it is left to force itself on, human nature must shudder at the prospect held. We should in vain look for an

JEFFERSONIAN PRINCIPLES

example in the Spanish deportation or deletion
of the Moors. This precedent would fall far
short of our case. — *Autobiography*. Vol. I,
pp. 68–69. [This bill was introduced in the
Virginia legislature in 1779 in connection with
the revision of the laws. Jefferson was a
member of the committee in charge. — Ed.]

[In the revision of the Virginia state laws in
1779 Jefferson proposed] "to emancipate all
slaves born after passing the act. The bill
reported by the revisers does not itself contain
this proposition; but an amendment containing
it was prepared, to be offered to the legislature
whenever the bill should be taken up, and
further directing that they should continue
with their parents to a certain age, then be
brought up, at the public expence, to tillage,
arts, or sciences, according to their geniusses,
till the females should be eighteen, and the
males twenty-one years of age, when they
should be colonized to such place as the circumstances of the time should render most
proper, sending them out with arms, ammuni-
tion, implements of houshold and of the
handicraft arts, seeds, pairs of the useful
domestic animals, &c. to declare them a free

JEFFERSONIAN PRINCIPLES

and independent people, and extend to them
our alliance and protection, till they shall have
acquired strength; and to send vessels at the
same time to other parts of the world for an
equal number of white inhabitants; to induce
whom to migrate hither, proper encouragements
were to be proposed. It will probably be asked,
Why not retain and incorporate the blacks into
the state, and thus save the expence of supply-
ing by importation of white settlers, the
vacancies they will leave? Deep rooted prejudices entertained by the whites; ten thousand
recollections by the blacks, of the injuries they
have sustained; new provocations; the real
distinctions which nature has made; and many
other circumstances will divide us into parties,
and produce convulsions, which will probably
never end but in the extermination of the one or
the other race. — To these objections, which
are political, may be added others, which are
physical and moral." — *Notes on Virginia.*
Vol. III, pp. 243–244.

On Parties and Secession

In every free and deliberating society, there
must, from the nature of man, be opposite
parties, and violent dissensions and discords;

and one of these, for the most part, must prevail over the other for a longer or shorter time. Perhaps this party division is necessary to induce each to watch and delate to the people the proceedings of the other. But if on a temporary superiority of the one party, the other is to resort to a scission of the Union, no federal government can ever exist. If to rid ourselves of the present rule of Massachusetts and Connecticut, we break the Union, will the evil stop there? Suppose the New England States alone cut off, will our nature be changed? Are we not men still to the south of that, with all the passions of men? Immediately, we shall see a Pennsylvania and a Virginia party arise in the residuary confederacy, and the public mind will be distracted with the same party spirit. What a game too will the one party have in their hands, by eternally threatening the other that unless they do so and so, they will join their northern neighbors. If we reduce our Union to Virginia and North Carolina, immediately the conflict will be established between the representatives of these two States, and they will end by breaking into their simple units. Seeing, therefore, that an association of men who will not quarrel with one another is a thing which never yet existed, from the greatest confederacy of nations down to a town meeting or a vestry; seeing that we must have somebody to quarrel with, I had rather keep our New England associates for that purpose, than to see our bickerings transferred to others. They are circumscribed within such narrow limits, and their population so full, that their numbers will ever be the minority, and they are marked, like the Jews, with such a perversity of character, as to constitute, from that circumstance, the natural division of our parties. A little patience, and we shall see the reign of witches pass over, their spells dissolved, and the people recovering their true sight, restoring their government to its true principles. It is true, that in the meantime, we are suffering deeply in spirit, and incurring the horrors of a war, and long oppressions of enormous public debt. But who can say what would be the evils of a scission, and when and where they would end? Better keep together as we are, haul off from Europe as soon as we can, and from all attachments to any portions of it; and if they show their power just sufficiently to hoop us together, it will be the happiest situation in which we can exist. — *Letter to*

JEFFERSONIAN PRINCIPLES

John Taylor, June 1, 1798.   Vol. VII, pp. 264–265.

ON REBELLION

Yet where does this anarchy exist? Where did it ever exist, except in the single instance of Massachusetts?[1] And can history produce an instance of rebellion so honourably conducted? I say nothing of it's motives. They were founded in ignorance, not wickedness. God forbid we should ever be 20 years without such a rebellion. The people cannot be all, & always, well informed. The part which is wrong will be discontented in proportion to the importance of the facts they misconceive. If they remain quiet under such misconceptions it is a lethargy, the forerunner of death to the public liberty. We have had 13 states independent 11 years. There has been one rebellion. That comes to one rebellion in a century and a half for each state. What country before ever existed a century and a half without a rebellion? & what country can preserve it's liberties if their rulers are not warned from time to time that their people preserve the spirit of resistance? Let them take arms. The remedy is to set them

[1] This refers to Shays's Rebellion.

right as to facts, pardon & pacify them. What signify a few lives lost in a century or two? The tree of liberty must be refreshed from time to time with the blood of patriots & tyrants. It is it's natural manure. — *Letter to William S. Smith*, November 13, 1787. Vol. IV, p. 467.

Societies exist under three forms sufficiently distinguishable. 1. Without government, as among our Indians. 2. Under governments wherein the will of every one has a just influence, as is the case in England in a slight degree, and in our states, in a great one. 3. Under governments of force: as is the case in all other monarchies and in most of the other republics. To have an idea of the curse of existence under these last, they must be seen. It is a government of wolves over sheep. It is a problem, not clear in my mind, that the 1st condition is not the best. But I believe it to be inconsistent with any great degree of population. The second state has a great deal of good in it. The mass of mankind under that enjoys a precious degree of liberty & happiness. It has it's evils too: the principal of which is the turbulence to which it is subject. But weigh this against the oppressions of monarchy, and it becomes nothing. *Malo periculosam libertatem quam quietam servitutem.* Even this evil is productive of good. It prevents the degeneracy of government, and nourishes a general attention to the public affairs. I hold it that a little rebellion now and then is a good thing, & as necessary in the political world as storms in the physical. Unsuccessful rebellions indeed generally establish the encroachments on the rights of the people which have produced them. An observation of this truth should render honest republican governors so mild in their punishment of rebellions, as not to discourage them too much. It is a medicine necessary for the sound health of government. — *Letter to James Madison*, January 30, 1787. Vol. IV, pp. 362–363.

On Naturalization

I cannot omit recommending a revisal of the laws on the subject of naturalization. Considering the ordinary chances of human life, a denial of citizenship under a residence of fourteen years is a denial to a great proportion of those who ask it, and controls a policy pursued from the first settlement by many of these States, and still believed of consequence to their prosperity. And shall we refuse the unhappy fugitives from distress that hospitality which the savages of the wilderness extended to our fathers arriving in this land? Shall oppressed humanity find no asylum on this globe? The constitution, indeed, has wisely provided that, for admission to certain offices of important trust, a residence shall be required sufficient to develop character and design. But might not the general character and capabilities of a citizen be safely communicated to every one manifesting a *bona fide* purpose of embarking his life and fortunes permanently with us? with restrictions, perhaps, to guard against the fraudulent usurpation of our flag; an abuse which brings so much embarrassment and loss on the genuine citizen, and so much danger to the nation of being involved in war, that no endeavor should be spared to detect and suppress it. — *First annual message to Congress,* December 8, 1801. Vol. VIII, p. 124.

On Excluding Europe from the Americas

The truth is that the patriots of Spain have no warmer friends than the administration of the U. S., but it is our duty to say nothing & to do nothing for or against either. If they succeed, we shall be well satisfied to see Cuba & Mexico remain in their present dependence; but very unwilling to see them in that of either France or England, politically or commercially. We consider their [Cuban and Mexican] interests & ours as the same, and that the object of both must be to exclude all European influence from this hemisphere. — *Letter to the Governor of Louisiana*, October 29, 1808. Vol. IX, p. 212.

On the Monroe Doctrine

The question presented by the letters you have sent me, is the most momentous which has ever been offered to my contemplation since that of Independence. That made us a nation, this sets our compass and points the course which we are to steer through the ocean of time opening before us. And never could we embark on it under circumstances more auspicious. Our first and fundamental maxim should be, never to entangle ourselves in the broils of Europe. Our second, never to suffer Europe to intermeddle with cis-Atlantic affairs. America, North and South, has a set of interests distinct from those of Europe, and peculiarly her own. She should therefore have a system of her own, separate and apart from that of

JEFFERSONIAN PRINCIPLES

Europe. While the last is laboring to become
the domicile of despotism, our endeavor should
surely be, to make our hemisphere that of freedom. One nation, most of all, could disturb us
in this pursuit; she now offers to lead, aid, and
accompany us in it. By acceding to her
proposition, we detach her from the bands,
bring her mighty weight into the scale of free
government, and emancipate a continent at a
stroke, which might otherwise linger in doubt
and difficulty. Great Britain is the nation
which can do us the most harm of any one, or
all the earth; and with her on our side we need
not fear the whole world. With her then, we
should most sedulously cherish a cordial friendship; and nothing would tend more to knit our
affections than to be fighting once more, side
by side, in the same cause. — *Letter to James
Madison*, October 24, 1823. Vol. X, p. 277.

On France

I cannot leave this great and good country
without expressing my sense of it's preeminence
of character among the nations of the earth.
A more benevolent people, I have never known,
nor greater warmth & devotedness in their
select friendships. Their kindness and accomo-

dation to strangers is unparalleled, and the hospitality of Paris is beyond anything I had conceived to be practicable in a large city. Their eminence too in science, the communicative dispositions of their scientific men, the politeness of the general manners, the ease and vivacity of their conversation, give a charm to their society to be found nowhere else. In a comparison of this with other countries we have the proof of primacy, which was given by Themistocles after the battle of Salamis. Every general voted to himself the first reward of valor, and the second to Themistocles. So ask the travelled inhabitant of any nation, In what country on earth would you rather live? — Certainly in my own, where are all my friends, my relations, and the earliest & sweetest affections and recollections of my life. Which would be your second choice? France. — *Autobiography*. Vol. I, p. 149.

On Congressional Debate

I served with General Washington in the legislature of Virginia before the Revolution, and, during it, with Dr. Franklin in Congress. I never heard either of them speak ten minutes at a time, nor to any but the main point which was to decide the question. They laid their shoulders to the great points, knowing that the little ones would follow of themselves. If the present Congress errs in too much talking, how can it be otherwise in a body to which the people send 150 lawyers, whose trade it is to question everything, yielding nothing, & talk by the hour? That 150 lawyers should do business together ought not to be expected. — *Autobiography.* Vol. I, p. 82.

On Newspapers

To your request of my opinion of the manner in which a newspaper should be conducted, so as to be most useful, I should answer, "by restraining to true facts & sound principles only." Yet I fear such a paper would find few subscribers. It is a melancholy truth, that a suppression of the press could not more compleatly deprive the nation of it's benefits, than is done by it's abandoned prostitution to falsehood. Nothing can now be believed which is seen in a newspaper. Truth itself becomes suspicious by being put into that polluted vehicle. The real extent of this state of misinformation is known only to those who are in situations to confront facts within their knowledge with the lies of the day. I really look with commiseration over the great body of my fellow citizens, who, reading newspapers, live & die in the belief, that they have known something of what has been passing in the world in their time; whereas the accounts they have read in newspapers are just as true a history of any other period of the world as of the present, except that the real names of the day are affixed to their fables. General facts may indeed be collected from them, such as that Europe is now at war, that Bonaparte has been a successful warrior, that he has subjected a great portion of Europe to his will, &c., &c.; but no details can be relied on. I will add, that the man who never looks into a newspaper is better informed than he who reads them; inasmuch as he who knows nothing is nearer to truth than he whose mind is filled with falsehoods & errors. He who reads nothing will still learn the great facts, and the details are all false. . . .

Defamation is becoming a necessary of life; insomuch that a dish of tea in the morning or evening cannot be digested without this stimulant. Even those who do not believe these abominations, still read them with complaisance to their auditors, and instead of the abhorrence

& indignation which should fill a virtuous mind, betray a secret pleasure in the possibility that some may believe them, tho they do not themselves. It seems to escape them, that it is not he who prints, but he who pays for printing a slander, who is it's real author.—*Letter to John Norvell,* June 14, 1807. Vol. IX, pp. 73–74.

On the Freedom of the Press

No government ought to be without censors: & where the press is free, no one ever will. If virtuous, it need not fear the fair operations of attack & defence. Nature has given to man no other means of sifting out the truth either in religion, law, or politics. I think it as honorable to the government neither to know, nor notice, it's sycophants or censors, as it would be undignified & criminal to pamper the former & persecute the latter. — *Letter to President Washington,* September 9, 1792. Vol. VI, p. 108.

During the course of this administration, and in order to disturb it, the artillery of the press has been levelled against us, charged with whatsoever its licentiousness could devise or dare. These abuses of an institution so important to freedom and science, are deeply to be regretted, inasmuch as they tend to lessen its usefulness, and to sap its safety; they might, indeed, have been corrected by the wholesome punishments reserved and provided by the laws of the several States against falsehood and defamation; but public duties more urgent press on the time of public servants, and the offenders have therefore been left to find their punishment in the public indignation.

Nor was it uninteresting to the world, that an experiment should be fairly and fully made, whether freedom of discussion, unaided by power, is not sufficient for the propagation and protection of truth — whether a government, conducting itself in the true spirit of its constitution, with zeal and purity, and doing no act which it would be unwilling the whole world should witness, can be written down by falsehood and defamation. The experiment has been tried; you have witnessed the scene; our fellow citizens have looked on, cool and collected, they saw the latent source from which these outrages proceeded; they gathered around these public functionaries, and when the constitution called them to the decision by the suffrage, they pronounced their verdict, honorable to those who had served them, and consolatory to the friend of man, who believes he may be intrusted with his own affairs.

No inference is here intended, that the laws, provided by the State against false and defamatory publications, should not be enforced. He who has time, renders a service to public morals and public tranquillity, in reforming these abuses by the salutary coercions of the law, but the experiment is noted, to prove that, since truth and reason have maintained their ground against false opinions in league with false facts, the press, confined to truth, needs no other legal restraint; the public judgment will correct false reasonings and opinions, on a full hearing of all parties; and no other definite line can be drawn between the inestimable liberty of the press and its demoralizing licentiousness. If there be still improprieties which this rule would not restrain, its supplement must be sought in the censorship of public opinion. — *Second Inaugural Address*, March 4, 1805. Vol. VIII, p. 346.

On Defamation of Public Characters

It is really to be lamented that after a public servant has passed a life in important and faithful services, after having given the most plenary satisfaction in every station, it should yet be in the power of every individual to disturb his quiet, by arraigning him in a gazette and by obliging him to act as if he needed a defence, an obligation imposed on him by unthinking minds which never give themselves the trouble of seeking a reflection unless it be presented to them. However it is a part of the price we pay for liberty, which cannot be guarded but by the freedom of the press, nor that be limited without danger of losing it. To the loss of time, of labour, of money, then, must be added that of quiet, to which those must offer themselves who are capable of serving the public, and all this is better than European bondage. — *Letter to John Jay*, January 25, 1786. Vol. IV, p. 186.

On Calumny in Public Life

At a very early period of my life, I determined never to put a sentence into any newspaper. I have religiously adhered to the resolution through my life, and have great reason to be contented with it. Were I to undertake to answer all the calumnies of the newspapers, it would be more than all my own time, & that of 20. aids could effect. I have thought it better to trust to the justice of my countrymen, that they would judge me by what they *see* of my conduct on the stage where they have placed me, & what they knew of me *before* the epoch since which a particular party has supposed it might answer some views of theirs to vilify me in the public eye. Some, I know, will not reflect how apocryphal is the testimony of enemies so palpably betraying the views with which they give it. But this is an injury to which duty requires every one to submit whom the public think proper to call into it's councils. I thank you, my dear Sir, for the interest you have taken for me on this occasion. Though I have made up my mind not to suffer calumny to disturb my tranquillity, yet I retain all my sensibilities for the approbation of the good & just. — *Letter to Samuel Smith*, August 22, 1798. Vol. VII, p. 279.

On Making Public Appointments

There are no offices in my gift but of meer [*sic*] scribes in the office room at 800. & 500. Dollars a year. These I found all filled & of long possession in the hands of those who held them, and I thought it would not be just to remove persons in possession, who had behaved well, to make place for others. . . . I am sensible of the necessity as well as justice of dispersing emploiments over the whole of the U. S. But this is difficult as to the smaller offices, which require to be filled immediately, as they become vacant & are not worth coming for from distant states. Hence they will unavoidably get into the sole occupation of the vicinities of the seat of government. — *Letter to Colonel Henry Lee*, April 26, 1790. Vol. V, p. 163. [Jefferson had just become Secretary of State. — Ed.]

With regard to appointments, I have so much confidence in the justice and good sense of the federalists, that I have no doubt they will concur in the fairness of the position, that after they have been in the exclusive possession of all offices from the very first origin of party among us, to the 3d of March, at 9 o'clock in the night, no republican ever admitted, & this doctrine newly avowed, it is now perfectly just that the republicans should come in for the vacancies which may fall in, until something like an equilibrium in office be restored; after which "Tros Tyriusque nullo discrimine habetur." But the great stumbling block will be removals, which tho' made on those just principles only on which my predecessor ought to have removed the same persons, will nevertheless be ascribed to removal on party principles. Imprimis. I will expunge the effects of Mr. A[dams]'s indecent conduct in crowding nominations after he knew they were not for himself, till 9 o'clock of the night, at 12 o'clock of which he was to go out of office. . . .2d. Some removals must be made for misconduct. — *Letter to Dr. Benjamin Rush*, March 24, 1801. Vol. VIII, pp. 31–32.

There are there [New York] 3. distinct sections of republicans. You know them without my venturing a specification of them through the post. I have the confidential sentiments of the most respectable persons of each. Two of these sections disapprove of removal but on a very small scale indeed. The other has opened a battery on us as you will see by the inclosed paper. You will be at no loss for the source of this. We shall yield a little to their pressure, but no more than appears absolutely necessary to keep them together. And if that would be as much as to disgust other parts of the union, we must prefer the greater to the lesser part. In Connecticut alone a general sweep seems to be called for on principles of justice and policy. Their legislature now sitting are removing every republican even from the commissions of the peace and the lowest offices. There then we will retaliate. Whilst the Federals are taking possession of all the state offices, exclusively, they ought not to expect we will leave them the exclusive possession of those at our disposal. The republicans have some rights : and must be protected.—*Letter to Wilson Cary Nicholas*, June 11, 1801.   Vol. VIII, pp. 64-65.

When it is considered, that during the late administration, those who were not of a particular sect of politics were excluded from all office; when, by a steady pursuit of this measure, nearly the whole offices of the U. S. were monopolized by that sect; when the public sentiment at length declared itself, and burst open the doors of honor and confidence to those whose opinions they more approved, was it to be imagined that this monopoly of office was still to be continued in the hands of the minority? Does it violate their *equal rights*, to assert some rights in the majority also? Is it *political intolerance* to claim a proportionate share in the direction of public affairs? . . .

The remonstrance laments "that a change in the administration must produce a change in the subordinate officers;" in other words, that it should be deemed necessary for all officers to think with their principal. But on whom does this imputation bear? On those who have been so excluded? I lament sincerely that unessential differences of political opinion should ever have been deemed sufficient to interdict half the society from the rights and blessings of self-government, to proscribe them as characters unworthy of every trust. It would have been to me a circumstance of great relief, had I found a moderate participation of office in the hands of the majority. I would gladly have left to time and accident to raise them to their just share. But their total exclusion calls for prompter correctives. I shall correct the procedure; but that done, disdain to follow it, shall return with joy to that state of things, when the only questions concerning a candidate shall be, is he honest? Is he capable? Is he faithful to the Constitution? — *Letter to a Committee of the Merchants of New Haven,* July 12, 1801. Vol. VIII, pp. 69–70.

JEFFERSONIAN PRINCIPLES

Many vacancies have been made by death and resignation, many by removal for malversation in office and for open, active and virulent abuse of official influence in opposition to the order of things established by the will of the nation. Such removals continue to be made on sufficient proof. The places have been steadily filled with republican characters until of 316 offices in all the U. S. subject to appointment and removal by me, 130 only are held by federalists. . . . And this has been effected in little more than two years by means so moderate and just as cannot fail to be approved in future. Whether a participation of office in proportion to numbers should be effected in each state separately or in the whole states taken together is difficult to decide, and has not yet been settled in my own mind. It is a question of vast complications. — *Letter to William Duane*, July 24, 1803. Vol. VIII, p. 258.

It is rare that the public sentiment decides immorally or unwisely, and the individual who differs from it ought to distrust and examine well his own opinion. As to the character of the appointments which have been, & will be made,

JEFFERSONIAN PRINCIPLES

I have less to fear as to the satisfaction they will give, provided the real appointments only be attended *to*, and not the lying ones of which the papers are daily full. . . . But as to removals from office, great differences of opinion exist. That some ought to be removed all will agree. That all should, nobody will say: And no two will probably draw the same line between these two extremes; consequently nothing like general approbation can be expected. Mal-conduct is a just ground of removal: mere difference of political opinion is not. The temper of some states requires a stronger pro-cedure, that of others would be more alienated even by a milder course. — *Letter to William Findley*, March 24, 1801. Vol. VIII, p. 27. [Jefferson was then beginning his term as President. — Ed.]

On His Distaste for Public Life

If the public then has no claim on me, & my friends nothing to justify; the decision [of remaining in public life] will rest on my own feelings alone. There has been a time when these were very different from what they are now: when perhaps the esteem of the world was of higher value in my eye than everything

in it. But age, experience & reflection, preserving to that only it's due value, have set a
higher on tranquility. The motion of my blood
no longer keeps time with the tumult of the
world. It leads me to seek for happiness in the
lap and love of my family, in the society of my
neighbors & my books, in the wholesome
occupations of my farm & my affairs, in an
interest or affection in every bud that opens,
in every breath that blows around me, in an
entire freedom of rest or motion, of thought or
incognitancy, owing account to myself alone of
my hours & actions. What must be the principle of that calculation which should balance
against these the circumstances of my present
existence! worn down with labours from morning to night, & day to day; knowing them as
fruitless to others as they are vexatious to
myself, committed singly in desperate & eternal
contest against a host who are systematically
undermining the public liberty & prosperity,
even the rare hours of relaxation sacrificed to
the society of persons, of whose hatred I am
conscious even in those moments of conviviality
when the heart wishes most to open itself to
the effusions of friendship and confidence, cut
off from my family & friends, my affairs

JEFFERSONIAN PRINCIPLES

abandoned to chaos & derangement, in short
giving everything I love, in exchange for
everything I hate, and all this without a single
gratification in possession or prospect, in
present enjoyment or future wish. — *Letter to
James Madison*, June 9, 1793. Vol. VI, pp.
291–292.

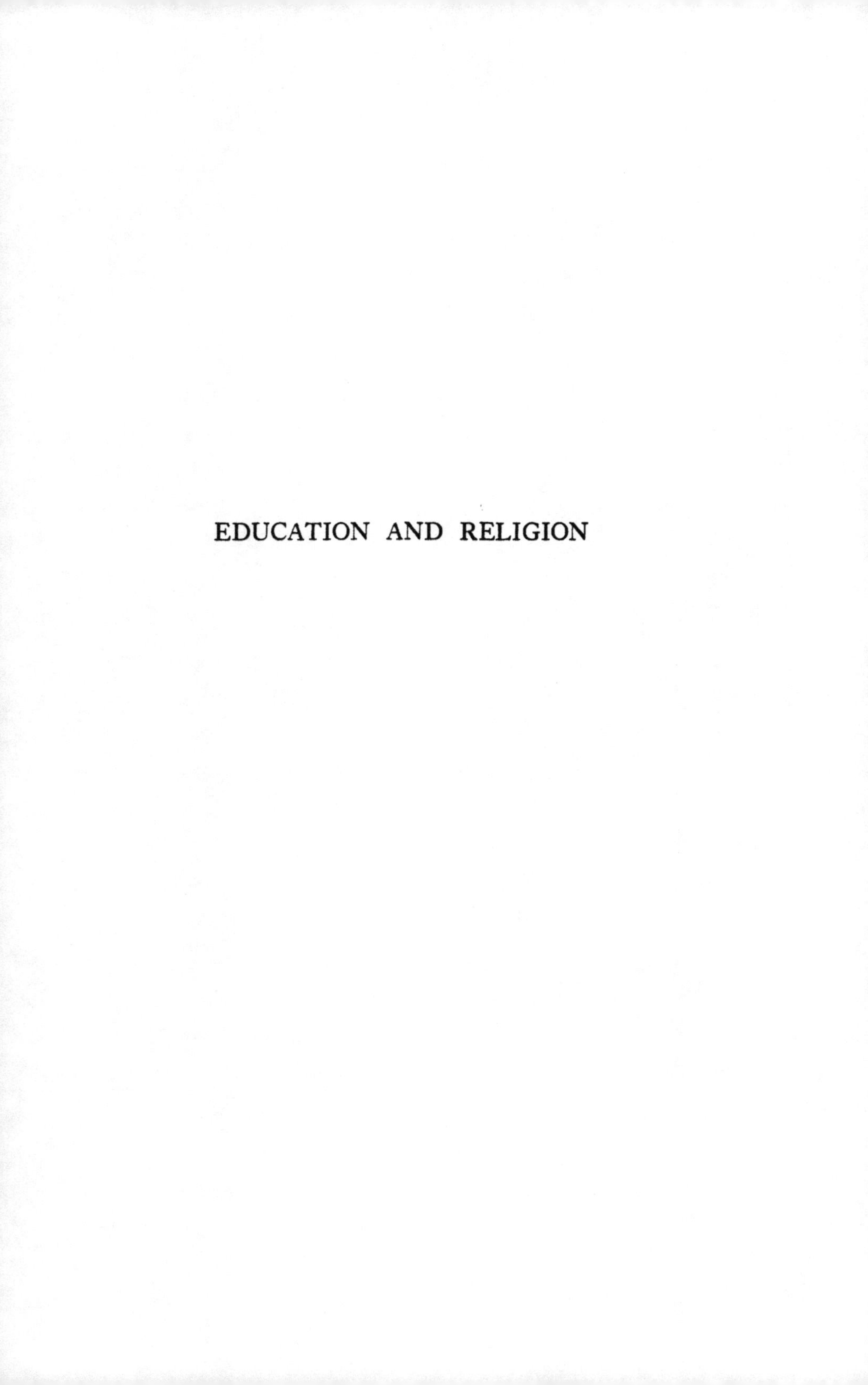

EDUCATION AND RELIGION

EDUCATION AND RELIGION

On Education

A LONGER race through life may have entitled me to seize some truths which have not yet been presented to your observation & more intimate knowledge of the country in which you are to live & of the circumstances in which you will be placed, may enable me to point your attention to the branches of science which will administer the most to your happiness there. The foundations which you have laid in languages and mathematics are proper for every superstructure. The former exercises our memory while that and no other faculty is yet matured & prevents our acquiring habits of idleness. The latter gives exercise to our reason, as soon as that has acquired a certain degree of strength, and stores the mind with truths which are useful in other branches of science. At this moment then a second order of preparation is to commence. I shall propose to you that it be extensive, comprehending Astronomy, Natural Philosophy (or Physics),

Natural History, Anatomy, Botany & Chemistry. No inquisitive mind will be content to be ignorant of any of these branches. But I would advise you to be contented with a course of lectures in most of them, without attempting to make yourself master of the whole. This is more than any genius joined to any length of life is equal to. You will find among them some one study to which your mind will more particularly attach itself. This then I would pursue & propose to attain eminence in. . . . You will find botany offering it's charms to you at every step. . . . Beside the comfort of knowledge, every science is auxiliary to every other. While you are attending these courses you can proceed by yourself in a regular series of historical reading. It would be a waste of time to attend a professor of this. It is to be acquired from books and if you pursue it by yourself you can accomodate it to your other reading so as to fill up those chasms not otherwise appropriated. There are portions of the day too when the mind should be eased, particularly after dinner it should be applied to lighter occupation : history is of this kind. It exercises principally the memory. Reflection also indeed is necessary but not generally in a laborious degree. To conduct yourself in this branch of science you have only to consider what areas of it merit a grasp & what a particular attention, & in each area also to distinguish between the countries the knowledge of whose history will be useful & those where it suffices only to be not altogether ignorant. Having laid down your plan as to the branches of history you would pursue, the order of time will be your sufficient guide. . . . The histories of Greece and Rome are worthy a good degree of attention, they should be read in the original authors. The transition from antient to modern history will be best effected by reading Gibbon's. Then a general history of the principal states of Europe, but particular ones of England. Here too the original writers are to be preferred. . . . After the history of England that of America will claim your attention. Here too original authors & not compilers are best. An author who writes of his own times or of times near his own presents in his own ideas & manner the best picture of the moment of which he writes. . . . When you shall have got thro this second order of preparation the study of the law is to be begun. This like history is to be acquired from books. All the aid you will want will be a catalogue of the books to be read & the order in which they are to be read. It being absolutely indifferent in what place you carry on this reading I should propose your doing it in France. The advantages of this will be that you will at the same time acquire the habit of speaking French which is the object of a year or two. You may be giving attention to such of the fine arts as your turn may lead you & you will be forming an acquaintance with the individuals & characters of a nation with whom we must long remain in the closest intimacy & to whom we are bound by the strong ties of gratitude and policy. A nation in short of the most amiable dispositions on earth, the whole mass of which is penetrated with an affection for us. You might before you return to your own country make a visit to Italy also.

I should have performed the office of but half a friend were I to confine myself to the improvement of the mind only. Knowledge indeed is a desirable, a lovely possession, but I do not scruple to say that health is more so. It is of little consequence to store the mind with science if the body be permitted to become debilitated. If the body be feeble, the mind will not be strong — the sovereign invigorator

JEFFERSONIAN PRINCIPLES

of the body is exercise, and of all exercises walking is best. A horse gives but a kind of half exercise, and a carriage is no better than a cradle. No one knows, till he tries, how easily a habit of walking is acquired. . . . Not less than two hours a day should be devoted to exercise, and the weather should be little regarded. A person not sick will not be injured by getting wet. . . . Brute animals are the most healthy, & they are exposed to all weather, and, of men, those are healthiest who are the most exposed. The recipe of those two descriptions of beings is simple diet, exercise and the open air. — *Letter to Thomas Mann Randolph, Jr.*, August 27, 1786. Vol. IV, pp. 289–294.

Our post-revolutionary youth are born under happier stars than you and I were. They acquire all learning in their mother's womb, and bring it into the world ready made. The information of books is no longer necessary; and all knowledge which is not innate, is in contempt, or neglect at least. Every folly must run its round; and so, I suppose, must that of self-learning and self-sufficiency; of rejecting the knowledge acquired in past ages, and starting on the new ground of intuition.

JEFFERSONIAN PRINCIPLES

When sobered by experience, I hope our successors will turn their attention to the advantages of education. I mean of education on the broad scale, and not that of the petty *academies*, as they call themselves, which are starting up in every neighborhood, and where one or two men, possessing Latin and sometimes Greek, a knowledge of the globes, and the first six books of Euclid, imagine and communicate this as the sum of science. They commit their pupils to the theatre of the world, with just taste enough of learning to be alienated from industrious pursuits, and not enough to do service in the ranks of science. — *Letter to John Adams*, July 5, 1814. Vol. IX, p. 464.

On Public Education

I think by far the most important bill in our whole code is that for the diffusion of knowledge among the people. No other sure foundation can be devised, for the preservation of freedom and happiness. . . . Preach, my dear Sir, a crusade against ignorance; establish & improve the law for educating the common people. Let our countrymen know that the people alone can protect us against these evils,[1] and that the

[1] The miseries of the common people of France at that time.

tax which will be paid for this purpose is not more than the thousandth part of what will be paid to kings, priests & nobles who will rise up among us if we leave the people in ignorance. — *Letter to George Wythe*, August 13, 1786. Vol. IV, pp. 268–269.

On Education and Local Government

I have indeed two great measures at heart, without which no republic can maintain itself in strength.   1. That of general education, to enable every man to judge for himself what will secure or endanger his freedom.   2. To divide every county into hundreds, of such size that all the children of each will be within a central school in it. . . .   These little republics would be the main strength of the great one.   We owe to them the vigor given to our revolution in its commencement in the Eastern States. — *Letter to Governor Tyler*, May 26, 1810.   Quoted by J. S. Williams, *Thomas Jefferson*, p. 96.

There are two subjects, indeed, which I shall claim a right to further as long as I breathe, the public education, and the sub-division of counties into wards.   I consider the continuance of republican government as absolutely hanging on these two hooks. Of the first, you will, I am sure, be an advocate, as having already reflected on it, and of the last, when you shall have reflected. — *Letter to J. C. Cabell*, January 31, 1814. Vol. IX, p. 453.

ON THE OBJECTS OF PRIMARY EDUCATION

1. To give to every citizen the information he needs to transact his own business.
2. To enable him to calculate for himself and to express and preserve his ideas, contracts and accounts in writing.
3. To improve, by reading, his faculties and morals.
4. To understand his duties to his neighbors and his country, and to discharge with competence the functions confided to him by either.
5. To know his rights; to exercise with order and justice those he retains; to choose with discretion the fiduciary of those he delegates, and to notice their conduct with diligence, candor and judgment.
6. And, in general, to observe with intelligence and faithfulness all the social relations under which he shall be placed. — Quoted by J. S. Williams, *Thomas Jefferson*, p. 267.

JEFFERSONIAN PRINCIPLES

On Moral Philosophy

I think it lost time to attend lectures in this
branch. He who made us would have been a
pitiful bungler if he had made the rules of our
moral conduct a matter of science. For one
man of science, there are thousands who are
not. What would have become of them ? Man
was destined for society. His morality therefore was to be formed to this object. He was
endowed with a sense of right & wrong merely
relative to this. This sense is as much part of
his nature as the sense of hearing, seeing, feeling ;
it is the true foundation of morality, & not
the το καλον, truth, &c. as fanciful writers have
imagined. The moral sense, or conscience, is
as much a part of man as his leg or arm. It is
given to all human beings in a stronger or weaker
degree, as force of members is given them in a
greater or less degree. It may be strengthened
by exercise, as may any particular limb of the
body. This sense is submitted indeed in some
degree to the guidance of reason; but it is a
small stock which is required for this: even a
less one than what we call common sense.
State a moral case to a ploughman & a professor.
The former will decide it as well, & often

better than the latter, because he has not been led astray by artificial rules. In this branch therefore read good books because they will encourage as well as direct your feelings. The writings of Sterne particularly form the best course of morality that ever was written. Besides these read the books mentioned in the enclosed paper; and above all things lose no occasion to be generous, to be charitable, to be humane, to be true, just, firm, orderly, courageous &c. Consider every act of this kind as an exercise which will strengthen your moral faculties, & increase your worth. — *Letter to Peter Carr*, August 10, 1787. Vol. IV, pp. 428–429.

On Christ

The doctrines of Jesus are simple, and tend all to the happiness of man.

1. That there is one only God, and he all perfect.

2. That there is a future state of rewards and punishments.

3. That to love God with all thy heart and thy neighbor as thyself, is the sum of religion. These are the great points on which he endeavored to reform the religion of the Jews.

But compare with these the demoralizing dogmas of Calvin.

1. That there are three Gods.

2. That good works, or the love of our neighbor, are nothing.

3. That faith is every thing, and the more incomprehensible the proposition, the more merit in its faith.

4. That reason in religion is of unlawful use.

5. That God, from the beginning, elected certain individuals to be saved, and certain others to be damned; and that no crimes of the former can damn them; no virtues of the latter save.

Now, which of these is the true and charitable Christian? He who believes and acts on the simple doctrines of Jesus? Or the impious dogmatists, as Athanasius and Calvin? Verily I say these are the false shepherds foretold as to enter not by the door into the sheepfold, but to climb in some other way. They are mere usurpers of the Christian name, teaching a counter-religion made up of the *deliria* of crazy imaginations, as foreign from Christianity as is that from Mahomet. Their blasphemies have driven thinking men into infidelity, who have too hastily rejected the supposed author himself, with the horrors so falsely imputed to him. Had the doctrines of Jesus been preached always as pure as they came from his lips, the whole civilized world now would have been Christian. I rejoice that in this blessed country of free inquiry and belief, which has surrendered its creed and conscience to neither kings nor priests, the genuine doctrine of one only God is reviving, and I trust that there is not a *young man* now living in the United States who will not die an Unitarian.

But much I fear, that when this great truth shall be re-established, its votaries will fall into the fatal error of fabricating formulas of creed and confessions of faith, the engines which so soon destroyed the religion of Jesus, and made of Christendom a mere Aceldama. — *Letter to Dr. Benjamin Waterhouse*, June 26, 1822. Vol. X, pp. 219–220.

I rejoice that you have undertaken the task of comparing the moral doctrines of Jesus with those of the ancient Philosophers. You are so much in possession of the whole subject, that you will do it easier & better than any other person living. I think you cannot avoid giving, as preliminary to the comparison, a digest of his moral doctrines, extracted in his own words from the Evangelists, and leaving out everything relative to his personal history and character. It would be short and precious. With a view to do this for my own satisfaction, I had sent to Philadelphia to get two testaments Greek of the same edition, & two English, with a design to cut out the morsels of morality, and paste them on the leaves of a book, in the manner you describe as having been pursued in forming your Harmony. But I shall now get the thing done by better hands. — *Letter to Dr. Joseph Priestley*, January 29, 1804. Vol. VIII, p. 294.

ON CHRISTIANITY

In a comparative view of the Ethics of the enlightened nations of antiquity, of the Jews and of Jesus, no notice should be taken of the corruptions of reason among the ancients, to wit, the idolatry & superstition of the vulgar, nor of the corruptions of Christianity by the learned among its professors. . . .

I. Philosophers. 1. Their precepts related chiefly to ourselves, and the government of those passions which, unrestrained, would disturb our tranquillity of mind. In this branch of philosophy they were really great. 2. In developing our duties to others, they are short and defective. They embraced, indeed, the circles of kindred & friends, and inculcated patriotism, or the love of our country in the aggregate, as a primary obligation : toward our neighbors & countrymen they taught justice, but scarcely viewed them as within the circle of benevolence. Still less have they inculcated peace, charity & love to our fellow men, or embraced with benevolence the whole family of mankind.

II. Jews. 1. Their system was Deism; that is, the belief of one only God. But their ideas of him & of his attributes were degrading & injurious. 2. Their Ethics were not only imperfect, but often irreconciliable with the sound dictates of reason & morality, as they respect intercourse with those around us; & repulsive & anti-social respecting other nations. . . .

III. Jesus. In this state of things among the Jews, Jesus appeared. His parentage was obscure; his condition poor; his education null; his natural endowments great; his life correct and innocent : he was meek, benevolent, patient, firm, disinterested, & of the sublimest eloquence.

The disadvantages under which his doctrines appear are remarkable.

JEFFERSONIAN PRINCIPLES

1. Like Socrates & Epictetus, he wrote nothing himself.

2. But he had not, like them, a Xenophon or an Arrian to write for him. On the contrary, all the learned of his country, entrenched in its power and riches, were opposed to him — lest his labors should undermine their advantages; and the committing to writing his life & doctrines, fell on the most unlettered & ignorant men, who wrote, too, from memory, & not till long after the transactions had passed.

3. According to the ordinary fate of those who attempt to enlighten and reform mankind, he fell an early victim to the jealousy & combination of the altar and the throne, at about 33 years of age, his reason having not yet attained the *maximum* of its energy, nor the course of his preaching, which was but of 3 years at most, presented occasions for developing a complete system of morals.

4. Hence the doctrines which he really delivered were defective as a whole, and fragments only of what he did deliver have come to us mutilated, misstated, & often unintelligible.

5. They have been still more disfigured by the corruptions of schismatising followers, who

have found an interest in sophisticating & perverting the simple doctrines he taught by engrafting on them the mysticisms of a Grecian sophist, frittering them into subtleties, & obscuring them with jargon, until they have caused good men to reject the whole in disgust, & to view Jesus himself as an impostor.

Notwithstanding these disadvantages, a system of morals is presented to us, which, if filled up in the true style and spirit of the rich fragments he left us, would be the most perfect and sublime that has ever been taught by man.

The question of his being a member of the Godhead, or in direct communication with it, claimed for him by some of his followers, and denied by others, is foreign to the present view, which is merely an estimate of the intrinsic merit of his doctrines.

1. He corrected the Deism of the Jews, confirming them in their belief of one only God, and giving them juster notions of his attributes and government.

2. His moral doctrines, relating to kindred & friends, were more pure & perfect than those of the most correct of the philosophers, and greatly more so than those of the Jews; and they went far beyond both in inculcating uni-

versal philanthropy, not only to kindred and friends, to neighbors and countrymen, but to all mankind, gathering all into one family, under the bonds of love, charity, peace, common wants and common aids. . . .

3. The precepts of philosophy, & of the Hebrew code, laid hold of actions only. He pushed his scrutinies into the heart of man; erected his tribunal in the region of his thoughts — and purified the waters at the fountain head.

4. He taught, emphatically, the doctrines of a future state, which was either doubted, or disbelieved by the Jews; and wielded it with efficacy, as an important incentive, supplementary to the other motives to moral conduct. — *Syllabus of an Estimate of the Merit of the Doctrines of Jesus, Compared with Those of Others*, April, 1803. Drawn up for Benjamin Rush. Vol. VIII, pp. 223–228.

On Religion

I, too, have made a wee-little book from the same materials, which I call the Philosophy of Jesus; it is a pardigma of his doctrines, made by cutting the texts out of the book [the Bible], and arranging them on the pages of a blank book, in a certain order of time or subject. A more beautiful or precious morsel of ethics I have never seen; it is a document in proof that *I* am a *real Christian*, that is to say, a disciple of the doctrines of Jesus, very different from the Platonists, who call *me* infidel and *themselves* Christians and preachers of the gospel, while they draw all their characteristic dogmas from what its author never said or saw. They have compounded from the heathen mysteries a system beyond the comprehension of man, of which the great reformer of the various ethics and deism of the Jews, were he to return on earth, would not recognize one feature. — *Letter to Charles Thomson*, January 9, 1816. Vol. X, pp. 5–6.

As to myself, my religious reading has long been confined to the moral branch of religion, which is the same in all religions; while in that branch which consists of dogmas, all differ, all have a different set. The former instructs us how to live well and worthily in society; the latter are made to interest our minds in the support of teachers who inculcate them. Hence, for one sermon on a moral subject, you hear ten on the dogmas of the sect. However, religion is not the subject for you and me; neither of us know the religious opinions of the other; that is a matter between our Maker and ourselves. — *Letter to Thomas Leiper*, January 21, 1809. Vol. IX, p. 238.

The result of your fifty or sixty years of religious reading, in the four words, "Be just and good," is that in which all our inquiries must end; as the riddles of all the priesthoods end in four more, "*ubi panis, ibi deus.*" What we all agree in, is probably right. What no two agree in, most probably wrong. One of our fan-coloring biographers, who paints small men as very great, inquired of me lately, with real affection too, whether he might consider as authentic, the change of my religion much spoken of in some circles. Now this supposed that they knew what had been my religion before, taking for it the word of their priests, whom I certainly never made the confidants of my creed. My answer was, "say nothing of my religion. It is known to my God and myself alone. Its evidence before the world is to be sought in my life; if that has been *honest and dutiful* to society, the religion which has regulated it cannot be a bad one." — *Letter to John Adams*, January 11, 1817. Vol. X, p. 73.

JEFFERSONIAN PRINCIPLES

Your reason is now mature enough to examine this object. In the first place divest yourself of all bias in favour of novelty & singularity of opinion. Indulge them in any other subject rather than that of religion. It is too important, & the consequences of error may be too serious. On the other hand shake off all the fears & servile prejudices under which weak minds are servilely crouched. Fix reason firmly in her seat, and call to her tribunal every fact, every opinion. Question with boldness even the existence of a god; because, if there be one, he must more approve of the homage of reason, than that of blindfold fear. You will naturally examine first the religion of your own country. Read the bible then, as you would read Livy or Tacitus. The facts which are within the ordinary course of nature you will believe on the authority of the writer, as you do those of the same kind in Livy & Tacitus. The testimony of the writer weighs in their favor in one scale, and their not being against the laws of nature does not weigh against them. But those facts in the bible which contradict the laws of nature, must be examined with more care, and under a variety of faces. Here you must recur to the pretensions of the writer to inspiration from god. Examine upon what evidence his pretensions are founded, and whether that evidence is so strong as that its falsehood would be more improbable than a change in the laws of nature in the case he relates. . . . You will next read the new testament. It is the history of a personage called Jesus. Keep in your eye the opposite pretensions 1. of those who say he was begotten by god, born of a virgin, suspended & reversed the laws of nature at will, & ascended bodily into heaven: and 2. of those who say he was a man of illegitimate birth, of a benevolent heart, enthusiastic mind, who set out without pretensions to divinity, ended in believing them, & was punished capitally for sedition by being gibbetted according to the Roman law which punished the first commission of that offence by whipping, & the second by exile or death *in furca*. See this law in the Digest Lib. 48. tit. 19. #28. 3. & Lipsius Lib. 2. de cruce. cap. 2. These questions are examined in the books I have mentioned under the head of religion, & several others. They will assist you in your inquiries, but keep your reason firmly on the watch in reading them all. Do not be frightened from this inquiry by any fear of it's consequences. If it ends in a belief that there is no god, you will find incitements to virtue in the comfort & pleasantness you feel in it's exercise, and the love of others which it will procure you. If you find reason to believe there is a god, a consciousness that you are acting under his eye, & that he approves you, will be a vast additional incitement; if that there be a future state, the hope of a happy existence in that increases the appetite to deserve it; if that Jesus was also a god, you will be comforted by a belief in his aid and love. In fine, I repeat that you must lay aside all prejudice on both sides, & neither believe nor reject anything because and other persons, or description of persons have rejected or believed it. Your own reason is the only oracle given you by heaven, and you are answerable not only for the rightness but uprightness of the decision. I forgot to observe when speaking of the new testament that you should read all the histories of Christ, as well of those whom a council of ecclesiastics have decided for us to be Pseudo-evangelists, as those they named Evangelists. Because these Pseudo-evangelists pretended to inspiration as much as the others, and you are to judge their pretensions by your own reason, & not by the reason of those

JEFFERSONIAN PRINCIPLES

ecclesiastics. — *Letter to Peter Carr*, August 10, 1787.   Vol. IV, pp. 430-432.

We are not in a world ungoverned by the laws and the power of a superior agent.   Our efforts are in his hand, and directed by it; and he will give them their effect in his own time. — *Letter to David Barrow*, May 1, 1815.   Vol. IX, p. 516.

On Religion and Priesthoods

You judge truly that I am not afraid of the priests.   They have tried upon me all their various batteries, of pious whining, hypocritical canting, lying & slandering, without being able to give me one moment of pain.   I have contemplated their order from the Magi of the East to the Saints of the West, and I have found no difference of character, but of more or less caution, in proportion to their information or ignorance of those on whom their interested duperies were to be plaid off.   Their sway in New England is indeed formidable.   No mind beyond mediocrity dares there to develope itself.   If it does, they excite against it the public opinion which they command, & by little, but incessant and teasing persecutions, drive it from among them. Their present emigrations to the Western country are real flights from persecution, religious & political, but the abandonment of the country by those who wish to enjoy freedom of opinion leaves the despotism over the residue more intense, more oppressive. They are now looking to the flesh pots of the South and aiming at foothold there by their missionary teachers. They have lately come forward boldly with their plan to establish " *a qualified religious instructor* over every thousand souls in the U. S." And they seem to consider none as qualified but their own sect. — *Letter to Horatio Gates Spafford*, January 10, 1816. Vol. X, pp. 12–13.

On Religious Toleration

To compel a man to furnish contributions of money for the propagation of opinions which he disbelieves and abhors, is sinful and tyrannical; that even the forcing him to support this or that teacher of his own religious persuasion, is depriving him of the comfortable liberty of giving his contributions to the particular pastor whose morals he would make his pattern, and whose powers he feels most persuasive to righteousness; and is withdrawing from the ministry those temporary rewards, which proceeding from an approbation of their personal conduct, are an additional incitement to earnest and unremitting labours for the instruction of mankind; that our civil rights have no dependence on our religious opinions, any more than our opinions in physics or geometry; and therefore the proscribing any citizen as unworthy the public confidence by laying upon him an incapacity of being called to offices of trust or emolument, unless he profess or renounce this or that religious opinion, is depriving him injudiciously of those privileges and advantages to which, in common with his fellow-citizens, he has a natural right; that it tends also to corrupt the principles of that very religion it is meant to encourage, by bribing with a monopoly of worldly honours and emoluments, those who will externally profess and conform to it; that though indeed these are criminals who do not withstand such temptation, yet neither are those innocent who lay the bait in their way; that the opinions of man are not the object of civil government, nor under its jurisdiction; that to suffer the civil magistrate to intrude his powers into the field of opinion and to restrain the profession or propagation of principles on supposition of their ill tendency is a dangerous falacy, which at once destroys all religious liberty, because he being of course judge of that tendency will make his opinions the rule of judgment, and approve or condemn the sentiments of others only as they shall square with or suffer from his own; that it is time enough for the rightful purposes of civil government for its officers to interfere when principles break out into overt acts against peace and good order; and finally, that truth is great and will prevail if left to herself; that she is the proper and sufficient antagonist to error, and has nothing to fear from the conflict unless by human interposition disarmed of her natural weapons, free argument and debate; errors ceasing to be dangerous when it is permitted to contradict them. — *From the Bill establishing religious freedom, introduced by Jefferson in the Virginia Legislature,* June 13, 1779. It was not passed until 1786. Vol. II, pp. 238–239.

From the dissensions among sects themselves arises necessarily a right of chusing & necessity of deliberating to which we will conform, but if we chuse for ourselves, we must allow others to chuse also, & to reciprocally [*sic*]. This establishes religious liberty.

Why require those things in order to ecclesiastical communion which Christ does not require in order to life eternal? [*sic*] How can that be the church of Christ which excludes such persons from its communion as he will one day receive into the kingdom of heaven.

The arms of a religious society or church are exhortations, admonitions & advice, & ultimately expulsion or excommunication. This last is the utmost limit of power.

How far does the duty of toleration extend?

1. No church is bound by the duty of toleration to retain within her bosom obstinate offenders against her laws.

2. We have no right to prejudice another in his *civil* enjoyments because he is of another church. If any man err from the right way, it is his misfortune, no injury to thee; nor therefore art thou to punish him in the things of this life because thou supposeth he will be miserable in that which is to come — on the contrary according to the spirit of the gospel, charity, bounty, liberality is due to him.

Every church being free, no one can have

jurisdiction over another one, not even when the civil magistrate joins it. . . .

The care of every man's soul belongs to himself. But what if he neglect the care of it? Well what if he neglect the care of his health or estate, which more nearly relate to the state. Will the magistrate make a law that he shall not be poor or sick? Laws provide against injury from others; but not from ourselves. God himself will not save men against their wills. . . .

I cannot give up my guidance to the magistrate, because he knows no more of the way to heaven than I do, & is less concerned to direct me right than I am to go right. . . .

No man has *power* to let another prescribe his faith. Faith is not faith without believing. No man can conform his faith to the dictates of another. The life & essence of religion consists in the internal persuasion or belief of the mind. External forms of worship, when against our belief are hypocrisy & impiety. Rom. 14.23. " He that doubteth is damned, if he eat, because he eateth not of faith: for whatsoever is not faith, is sin. . . ."

Compulsion in religion is distinguished peculiarly from compulsion in every other thing. I may grow rich by art I am compelled to follow, I may recover health by medecines I am compelled to take against my own judgment, but I cannot be saved by a worship I disbelieve & abhor. . . .

Whatsoever is lawful in the Commonwealth, or permitted to the subject in the ordinary way, cannot be forbidden to him for religious uses : & whatsoever is prejudicial to the Commonwealth in their ordinary uses & therefore prohibited by the laws, ought not to be permitted to churches in their sacred rites. . . .

Truth will do well enough if left to shift for herself. She seldom has received much aid from the power of great men to whom she is rarely known & seldom welcome. She has no need of force to procure entrance into the minds of men. Error has indeed often prevailed by the assistance of power or force. Truth is the proper & sufficient antagonist to error. If anything pass in a religious meeting seditiously and contrary to the public peace, let it be punished in the same manner & no otherwise than as if it had happened in a fair or market. . . .

He [Locke] says "neither Pagan nor Mahomedan nor Jew ought to be excluded from the civil rights of the Commonwealth because of his religion." Shall we suffer a Pagan to deal with us and not suffer him to pray to his god? Why have Xns been distinguished above all people who have ever lived, for persecutions? Is it because it is the genius of their religion? No, it's genius is the reverse. It is refusing *toleration* to those of a different opinion which has produced all the bustles and wars on account of religion. It was the misfortune of mankind that during the darker centuries the Xn priests following their ambition and avarice combining with the magistrate to divide the spoils of the people, could establish the notion that schismatics might be ousted of their possessions and destroyed. This notion we have not yet cleared ourselves from. In this case no wonder the oppressed should rebel, & they will continue to rebel & raise disturbance until their civil rights are fully restored to them & all partial distinctions, exclusions & incapacitations removed. — *From among papers labeled " Scraps Early in the Revolution."* Vol. II, pp. 99–103.

JEFFERSONIAN PRINCIPLES

On Enforced Uniformity

It is a singular anxiety which some people have that we should all think alike. Would the world be more beautiful were all our faces alike? were our tempers, our talents, our tastes, our forms, our wishes, aversions and pursuits cast exactly in the same mould? If no varieties existed in the animal, vegetable or mineral creation, but all move strictly uniform, catholic & orthodox, what a world of physical and moral monotony would it be! These are the absurdities into which those run who usurp the throne of God and dictate to Him what He should have done. — *Letter to Charles Thomson*, January 29, 1817. Vol. X, p. 76.

THE ART OF LIVING

THE ART OF LIVING

On Looking Forwards Rather Than Backwards

THE Gothic idea that we are to look backwards instead of forwards for the improvement of the human mind, and to recur to the annals of our ancestors for what is most perfect in government, in religion & in learning, is worthy of those bigots in religion & government, by whom it has been recommended, & whose purposes it would answer. But it is not an idea which this country will endure; and the moment of their showing it is fast ripening. — *Letter to Joseph Priestley*, January 27, 1800. Vol. VII, p. 415.

On Travel

This makes men wiser, but less happy. When men of sober age travel, they gather knolege [*sic*] which they may apply usefully for their country, but they are subject ever after to recollections mixed with regret, their affections are weakened by being extended over more objects, & they learn new habits which cannot be gratified when they return home. Young men who travel are exposed to all these inconveniences in a higher degree, to others still more serious, and do not acquire that wisdom for which a previous foundation is requisite by repeated & just observations at home. The glare of pomp & pleasure is analogous to the motion of their blood, it absorbs all their affection & attention, they are torn from it as from the only good in this world, and return to their home as to a place of exile & condemnation. Their eyes are for ever turned back to the object they have lost, & it's recollection poisons the residue of their lives. Their first & most delicate passions are hackneyed on unworthy objects here, & they carry home only the dregs, insufficient to make themselves or anybody else happy. Add to this a habit of idleness, an inability to apply themselves to business is acquired & renders them useless to themselves & their country. These observations are founded in experience. There is no place where your pursuit of knoledge [*sic*] will be so little obstructed by foreign objects as in your own country, nor any wherein the virtues of the heart will be less exposed to be weakened. — *Letter*

JEFFERSONIAN PRINCIPLES

to Peter Carr, August 10, 1787. Vol. IV, pp. 432-433.

On Extravagance

Among many good qualities which my countrymen possess some of a different character, unhappily mix themselves. The most remarkable are indolence, extravagance, & infidelity to their engagements. Cure the two first, and the last would disappear, because it is a consequence of them, and not proceeding from want of morals. I know of no remedy against indolence & extravagance but a free course of justice. Everything else is merely palliative; but unhappily the evil has gained too generally the mass of the nation to leave the course of justice unobstructed. The maxim of buying nothing without the money in our pocket to pay for it, would make of our country one of the happiest upon earth. Experience during the war proved this; as I think every man will remember that under all the privations it obliged him to submit to during that period he slept sounder & awaked happier than he can do now. — *Letter to A. Donald*, July 28, 1787. Vol. IV, p. 414.

JEFFERSONIAN PRINCIPLES

On Lack of Time

No person will have occasion to complain of the want of time who never loses any. It is wonderful how much may be done if we are always doing. — *Letter to Martha Jefferson*, May 5, 1787. Vol. IV, p. 388.

On Indolence

Of all the cankers of human happiness none corrodes with so silent, yet so baneful an influence, as indolence. Body and mind both unemployed, our being becomes a burthen, and every object about us loathsome, even the dearest. Idleness begets ennui, ennui the hypochondriac, and that a diseased body. No laborious person was ever yet hysterical. Exercise and application produce order in our affairs, health of body and cheerfulness of mind, and these make us precious to our friends. It is while we are young that the habit of industry is formed. If not then, it never is afterwards. The fortune of our lives, therefore, depends on employing well the short period of youth. — *Letter to Martha Jefferson*, March 28, 1787. Vol. IV, p. 372.

JEFFERSONIAN PRINCIPLES

On Friendship

AN IMAGINARY DIALOGUE

Head. "Everything in this world is a matter of calculation. Advance then with caution, the balance in your hand. Put into one scale the pleasures which any object may offer; but put fairly into the other the pains which are to follow, & see which preponderates. The making an acquaintance is not a matter of indifference. When a new one is proposed to you, view it all round. Consider what advantages it presents, & to what inconveniences it may expose you. Do not bite at the bait of pleasure till you know there is no hook beneath it. The art of life is the art of avoiding pain: & he is the best pilot who steers clearest of the rocks & shoals with which he is beset. Pleasure is always before us; but misfortune is at our side: while running after that, this arrests us. The most effectual means of being secure against pain is to retire with ourselves, & to suffice for our own happiness. Those, which depend on ourselves, are the only pleasures a wise man will count on: for nothing is ours which another may deprive us of. Hence the inestimable value of intellectual pleasures. Ever in our power, always leading us to something new, never cloying, we ride serene & sublime above the concerns of this mortal world, contemplating truth & nature, matter & motion, the laws which bind up their existence, & that eternal being who made & bound them up by those laws. Let this be our employ. Leave the bustle & tumult of society to those who have not talents to occupy themselves without them. Friendship is but another name for an alliance with the follies & the misfortunes of others. Our own share of miseries is sufficient: why enter then as volunteers into those of another? Is there so little gall poured into our cup that we must needs help to drink that of our neighbor? A friend dies or leaves us: we feel as if a limb was cut off. He is sick: we must watch over him, & participate of his pains. His fortune is shipwrecked; ours must be laid under contribution. He loses a child, a parent, or a partner: we must mourn the loss as if it were our own.

Heart. And what more sublime delight than to mingle tears with one whom the hand of heaven hath smitten! to watch over the bed of sickness, & to beguile it's tedious & it's painful moments! to share our bread with one to whom misfortune has left none! This world abounds indeed with misery: to lighten it's burthen we must divide it with another. But let us try the virtues of your mathematical balance, & as you have put into one scales the burthen of friendship, let me put it's comforts into the other. When languishing then under disease, how grateful is the solace of our friends! how are we penetrated with their assiduities & attentions! how much are we supported by their encouragement & kind offices! When heaven has taken from us some object of our love, how sweet is it to have a bosom whereon to recline our heads, & into which we may pour the torrent of our tears! Grief, with such a comfort, is almost a luxury! In a life where we are perpetually exposed to want & accident, yours is a wonderful proposition, to insulate ourselves, to retire from all aid, & to wrap ourselves in the mantle of self-sufficiency! For assuredly nobody will care for him who cares for nobody. But friendship is precious, not only in the shade but in the sunshine of life; & thanks to a benevolent arrangement of things, the greater part of life is sunshine. . . . Let the gloomy monk, sequestered from the world, seek unsocial pleasures in the bottom of his cell! Let the sublimated philosopher grasp visionary happiness while pursuing phantoms dressed in the garb of truth! Their supreme wisdom is supreme folly; & they mistake for happiness the mere absence of pain. Had they ever felt the solid pleasure of one generous spasm of the heart, they would exchange for it all the frigid speculations of their lives, which you have been vaunting in such elevated terms. — *Dialogue between Head and Heart in letter to Mrs. Maria Cosway*, October 12, 1786. Vol. IV, pp. 317–319.

ON THE RULES OF GOOD SOCIETY

I have mentioned good humor as one of the preservatives of our peace & tranquillity. It is among the most effectual, and its effect is so well imitated and aided, artificially, by politeness, that this also becomes an acquisition of first rate value. In truth, politeness is artificial good humor, it covers the natural want of it, & ends by rendering habitual a substitute nearly equivalent to the real virtue. It is the practice of sacrificing to those whom we meet in society, all the little conveniences & preferences which will gratify them, & deprive us of nothing worth a moment's consideration; it is the giving a pleasing & flattering turn to our expressions, which will conciliate others, and make them pleased with us as well as themselves. How cheap a price for the good will of another! When this is in return for a rude thing said by another, it brings him to his senses, it mortifies & corrects him in the most salutary way, and places him at the feet of your good nature, in the eyes of the company. But in stating prudential rules for our government in society, I must not omit the important one of never entering into dispute or argument with another. I never saw the instance of two disputants convincing the other by argument. . . . Conviction is the effect of our own dispassionate reasoning, either in solitude, or weighing within ourselves, dispassionately, what we hear from others, standing uncommitted in argument ourselves. It was one of the rules which, above all others, made Doctor Franklin the most amiable of men in society, "never to contradict anybody." If he was urged to announce an opinion, he did it rather by asking questions, as if for information, or by suggesting doubts. . . . Good humor & politeness never introduce into mixed society, a question on which they foresee there will be a difference of

JEFFERSONIAN PRINCIPLES

opinion. — *Letter to Thomas Jefferson Randolph*,
November 24, 1808. Vol. IX, pp. 231–233.

On the Rules for Practical Life

1. Never put off till to-morrow what you can
   do to-day.
2. Never trouble another for what you can do
   for yourself.
3. Never spend your money before you have it.
4. Never buy what you do not want, because
   it is cheap; it will be dear to you.
5. Pride costs us more than hunger, thirst and
   cold.
6. We never repent of having eaten too little.
7. Nothing is troublesome that we do willingly.
8. How much pain have cost us the evils which
   have never happened.
9. Take things always by their smooth handle.
10. When angry, count ten, before you speak;
    if very angry, an hundred. — *Letter to
Thomas Jefferson Smith*, February 21, 1825.
Vol. X, p. 341.

JEFFERSONIAN PRINCIPLES

His Own Epitaph

———

HERE WAS BURIED
THOMAS JEFFERSON
AUTHOR
OF THE DECLARATION OF
AMERICAN INDEPENDENCE
OF
THE STATUTE OF VIRGINIA
FOR RELIGIOUS FREEDOM, AND
FATHER OF THE UNIVERSITY
OF VIRGINIA
BORN APRIL 2D
1743 O.S.
DIED [JULY 4]
[1826]

JEFFERSONIAN PRINCIPLES

ON ENFORCED UNIFORMITY

It is a singular anxiety which some people have that we should all think alike. Would the world be more beautiful were all our faces alike? were our tempers, our talents, our tastes, our forms, our wishes, aversions and pursuits cast exactly in the same mould? If no varieties existed in the animal, vegetable or mineral creation, but all move strictly uniform, catholic & orthodox, what a world of physical and moral monotony would it be! These are the absurdities into which those run who usurp the throne of God and dictate to Him what He should have done. — *Letter to Charles Thomson*, January 29, 1817. Vol. X, p. 76.